POCKET GUIDE TO ACCOMPANY MEDICAL ASSISTING

Administrative and Clinical Procedures Including Anatomy and Physiology

Kathryn A. Booth, RN-BSN, MS, RMA, RPT
Total Care Programming, Inc.
Palm Coast, Florida

Leesa G. Whicker, BA, CMA (AAMA)
Central Piedmont Community College
Charlotte, North Carolina

Terri D. Wyman, CMRS
UMass Memorial Medical Center
Worcester, Massachusetts

Donna Jeanne Pugh, RN, MSN/ED
University of Florida College of Nursing
Jacksonville, Florida

Sharion Thompson, BS, RMA
Bryant and Stratton College, Cleveland Area
Parma, Ohio

McGraw-Hill Higher Education

Boston   Burr Ridge, IL   Dubuque, IA   New York
San Francisco   St. Louis   Bangkok   Bogotá   Caracas   Kuala Lumpur
Lisbon   London   Madrid   Mexico City   Milan   Montreal   New Delhi
Santiago   Seoul   Singapore   Sydney   Taipei   Toronto

McGraw-Hill
Higher Education

POCKET GUIDE TO ACCOMPANY MEDICAL ASSISTING
Kathryn A. Booth, Leesa G. Whicker, Terri D. Wyman, Donna Jeanne
Pugh, and Sharion K. Thompson

Published by McGraw-Hill, a business unit of The McGraw-Hill
Companies, Inc., 1221 Avenue of the Americas, New York, NY 10020.

1 2 3 4 5 6 7 8 9 0 CSS/CSS 0 9 8

ISBN 978-0-07-325776-1
MHID 0-07-325776-1

Cover credits: *Applying lead wires: Kathryn Booth, Total Care
Programming, Inc.; Cover blood pressure: John Lund/Tiffany Schoepp,
©Gettyimages; DAQbilling® Practice Management Software screen
shots were provided by Antek HealthWare, LLC. www.antekhealthware
.com; background: David Gould, ©Gettyimages*

WARNING NOTICE: The clinical procedures, medicines, dosages,
and other matters described in this publication are based upon research
of current literature and consultation with knowledgeable persons in the
field. The procedures and matters described in this text reflect currently
accepted clinical practice. However, this information cannot and should
not be relied upon as necessarily applicable to a given individual's case.
Accordingly, each person must be separately diagnosed to discern the
patient's unique circumstances. Likewise, the manufacturer's package
insert for current drug product information should be consulted before
administering any drug. Publisher disclaims all liability for any inaccura-
cies, omissions, misuse, or misunderstanding of the information contained
in this publication. Publisher cautions that this publication is not intended
as a substitute for the professional judgment of trained medical personnel.

www.mhhe.com

Brief Contents

Section 1: Administrative

Section 2: Clinical

Section 3: General

Appendixes

Credits, Part 2

Pages 47–54, Dietary Supplements—Herbals and other substances: Reprinted courtesy of the National Institutes of Health.

Pages 54–56, Dietary Supplements— Vitamins and minerals: Reprinted courtesy of the Food and Drug Administration.

Pages 99–100, Immunization Schedule—Adolescent/Adult: Reprinted with the permission of the National Coalition of Adult Immunization.

Pages 100–102, Immunization Schedule—Child: Reprinted courtesy of the Centers for Disease Control.

Pages 106–107, Common Lab Tests (Waived Tests): Reprinted courtesy of the U.S. Department of Health and Human Services.

Page 173, Pregnancy Drug Risk Categories: Reprinted courtesy of the U.S. Drug Enforcement Administration.

Pages 196–197, Calories Burned During Activities: Adapted from Marvin R. Levy et al., *Life & Health: Targeting Wellness* (New York: McGraw-Hill, 1992).

Page 197, Food Label Terms: Reprinted courtesy of the U.S. Department of Agriculture and U.S. Department of Health and Human Services.

Pages 198–199, Saturated Fat and Cholesterol Sources: Reprinted courtesy of the U.S. Department of Agriculture.

Pages 199–200, Serving Sizes: Reprinted courtesy of the U.S. Department of Agriculture and U.S. Department of Health and Human Services.

Pages 222–223, Pulmonary Function—Tests: Adapted from *Illustrated Guide to Diagnostic Tests* (Springhouse, PA: Springhouse, 1998).

Contents/Index of Topics

Section 1: Administrative

Section 3: General

Anatomy and Physiology   243

Appendixes

1

Administrative

Appointment Scheduling

Appointment Scheduling Systems

- **Advance scheduling**—patients are given appointments well in advance
- **Cluster scheduling**—similar types of appointments are clustered together during the day or week
- **Combination scheduling**—a combination of more than one scheduling system is used
- **Double booking**—two or more patients are scheduled for the same appointment slot
- **Modified-wave**—similar to wave scheduling, patients arrive at scheduled intervals during an hour, allowing time to catch up before the next hour begins
- **Open-hours**—patients arrive at their own convenience and are seen on a first-come, first-served basis
- **Time-specified**—each patient is given an individual appointment time
- **Wave**—several patients are given the same appointment time beginning on the hour and are seen in the order they arrive; determine the number of patients per hour by dividing the hour by the average appointment length

Patient Information Needed to Schedule an Appointment

- Patient's full name
- Home and work telephone numbers
- Purpose of the visit

Scheduling Emergency Appointments

- Determine if an acute condition is an emergency based on office guidelines
- If unsure, ask the physician for instructions
- Adjust the schedule as necessary to accommodate patients with emergencies
- You may need to reschedule some patient appointments
- Let waiting patients know there is an emergency without giving details

Scheduling Hospital Surgery

1. Check the physician's schedule to see when she is scheduled to be in the operating room.
2. Call the operating room secretary. Give the procedure required, the name of the surgeon, the time involved, and the preferred date and hour.
3. Provide the patient's name (including birth name, if appropriate), address, telephone number, age, gender, patient identification number, and insurance information.
4. Call the admissions office. Arrange for the patient to be admitted on the day of surgery or the day before as indicated.

   Have the patient complete any preadmission ~rms the hospital requires.

   ~firm the surgery and the patient's arrival time ~ess day before surgery.

Typical Lengths of Common Procedures

Complete PE	30–60 minutes
New patient visit	30 minutes or more
Follow-up office visit	5–10 minutes
Emergency office visit	15–20 minutes
Prenatal exam	15 minutes
Pap smear and pelvic exam	15–30 minutes
Minor in-office surgery	30 minutes
Suture removal	10–20 minutes

Business Correspondence

Basic Rules of Writing

Capitalization

- All proper names
- All titles, positions, or indications of family relation when preceding a proper name or in place of a proper noun
- Days of the week, months, and holidays
- Names of organizations and membership designations
- Racial, religious, and political designations
- Adjectives, nouns, and verbs that are derived from proper nouns
- Specific addresses and geographic locations
- Sums of money written in legal or business documents
- Titles, headings of books, magazines newspapers

Numbers

Use numerals:

- In general writing, when the number is 11 or greater
- With abbreviations and symbols
- When discussing laboratory results or statistics
- When referring to specific sums of money
- When using a series of numbers in a sentence

Tips:

- Use commas when numerals have more than three digits
- Do not use commas when referring to account numbers, page numbers, or policy numbers
- Use a hyphen with numerals to indicate a range

Plurals

- Add *s* or *es* to most singular nouns
- With medical terms ending in *is*, drop the *is* and add *es*
- With terms ending in *um,* drop the *um* and add *a*
- With terms ending in *us,* drop the *us* and add *i*
- With terms ending in *a,* keep the *a* and add *e*

Possessives

To show ownership or relation to another noun:

For singular nouns, add an apostrophe and an *s*

For plural nouns that do not end in an *s*, add an apostrophe and an *s*

For plural nouns that end in an *s*, just add an apostrophe

Word division

Divide:

- According to pronunciation
- In compound words, between the two words from which they derive
- In hyphenated compound words, at the hyphen
- After a prefix
- Before a suffix
- Between two consonants that appear between vowels
- Before *-ing* unless the last consonant is doubled; in that case, divide before the second consonant

Do not divide:

- Suffixes such as *-sion, -tial,* and *-gion*
- A word so that only one letter is left on a line

Letter Styles

- **Full-Block**—all lines are flush left
- **Modified-Block**—similar to full block except that the dateline, complimentary closing, signature block, and notations are aligned at the center of the page or slightly to the right
- **Modified-Block with indented paragraphs**—identical to modified-block except that paragraphs are indented one-half inch
- **Simplified**—modification of full-block with omitted salutation and complimentary closing; includes a subject line and us open punctuation

Parts of a Letter

- **Margin**—the space around the edges of a form or letter that are left blank; the business standard is 1 inch
- **Letterhead**—the preprinted portion of business stationery
- **Dateline**—the month, day, year (for example, July 5, 2008); include it three lines below the letterhead on preprinted stationery
- **Inside Address**—the name and address of the person to whom the letter is being sent; place it two to four lines down from the date; include:
  - Courtesy title (Dr., Mr., Mrs., Ms.)
  - Company name if applicable
  - Numerals for street address, except the single numbers one through nine
    - Spell out numerical names of streets if less than ten
    - Spell out the words *Street, Drive,* etc.
  - Full city name
  - Two-letter USPS state abbreviation
    - Leave one space between the state and zip code
- **Salutation**—written greeting such as *Dear*
- **Subject Line**—information that brings the subject of the letter to the reader's attention
  - Place on second line below the salutation
    Place flush with left margin, indented
       spaces, or centered
          ˅de two or three words
             ˥ll capital letters

- **Body**—single-spaced text that is the largest part of the letter
  - Begin it two lines below the salutation or subject line
  - Double space between paragraphs
- **Complimentary Closing**—written closing; *Sincerely, Very truly yours,* or *Best regards* are acceptable business closings
  - Include it two lines below last line of the body
  - Capitalize the first letter only
- **Signature Block**—signature that includes the writer's name and business title
  - Align it with the complimentary closing
  - Include it three to four lines below the closing
  - Place the writer's name on the first line
  - Place the writer's business title on the second line
- **Identification Line**—the writer's initials followed by a colon or slash and the typist's initials
  - Include it flush left
  - Place it two lines below the signature block
- **Notations**—the number of enclosures included with the letter and the names of people receiving copies of the letter
  - Place it one or two lines below the identification line

Writing Tips

- Know the type of person to whom you are w:
- Know the purpose of the letter
- Be concise, clear, brief, and specific
- Do not use unnecessary words

- Use the active voice except when softening the tone of the letter
- Check spelling, grammar, and accuracy of dates and numbers

Charting and Documenting

6 Cs of Charting

- **Client's words**—record the exact words
- **Clarity**—use precise language
- **Completeness**—fill out the entire form
- **Conciseness**—be brief and to the point
- **Chronological order**—date entries in order
- **Confidentiality**—protect the patient's privacy

Ensuring the Doctor Can Find the Most Recent Patient Information

- Record all findings from exams and tests as soon as they are available
- Document telephone calls by recording the date and time of the call, who initiated it, the information discussed, and any conclusions or results
- Establish a procedure for retrieving a file quickly in case of emergency

Keeping Charts Neat and Easy to Read

- Use a good-quality pen that will not smudge or smear
- Use blue ink so that a photocopy is easily distinguished from the original
- attention to specific items with a highlighting

- Make sure handwriting is legible
- Use the proper procedure to correct the record

Coding Guidelines or Steps

Code Linkage

The procedural code should be linked to a diagnosis code. A code review should ensure that:

- Codes are appropriate to the patient profile
- Each code is billable
- A clear and correct linkage exists between procedure and diagnosis
- Payer's rules about diagnosis and procedures are followed
- Documentation in the patient's medical record supports the reported services
- Reported services comply with all regulations

Global Period

The period of time that is covered for follow-up care. The length of time will vary depending on the type of procedure performed.

Diagnostic Coding

Alphabetic index

- An index of the disease descriptions in the Tabular List
- An index in table format of drugs and chemicals that cause poisoning
- An index of external causes of injury, such as accidents

Code structure

- Diagnosis codes are made up of three, four, or five digits and a description
- The basic structure is three digits
- Adding the fourth and/or fifth digit makes the code more specific

Coding conventions

These symbols provide guidelines for using the code set

- **NOS**—not otherwise specified
- **NEC**—not elsewhere classified
- **[ ]** Brackets—used around synonyms, alternative wordings, or explanations
- **( )** Parentheses—used around descriptions that do not affect the code
- **:** Colon—used in the Tabular List after an incomplete term that needs one of the terms that follow to make it assignable to a given category
- **}** Brace—encloses a series of terms, each of which is modified by the statement that appears to the right of the brace
- **§** Section mark symbol—preceding a code, denotes the placement of a footnote at the bottom of the page that is applicable to all subdivisions in that code
- *Includes*—indicates that the entries following it refine the content of a preceding entry
- *Exclude*—indicates that an entry is not classified as part of the preceding code
- *Use additional code*—indicates that an additional code should be used, if available

- *Code first underlying disease*—appears when the category is not to be used as the primary diagnosis

Common diagnosis codes

Anxiety (generalized)	300.02
Bronchitis, acute	466.0
Cholesterolemia	272.0
Cough	786.2
Cough, smoker's	491.0
Depression, acute	296.2
Diabetes, NIDDM	250.00
Diabetes, IDDM	250.01
Diarrhea	787.91
Exam, adult physical	v70.0
Exam, child or infant	v20.2
Exam, sports, camp	v70.3
Fainting (syncope)	780.2
Fatigue	780.79
Fever	780.6
GERD (reflux)	530.81
Headache, tension	307.81
Headache, migraine—w/o intractable	346.1
Hypertension (benign)	401.0
Hypertension (essential malignant)	401.10
Hypothyroidism (NOS)	242.90
IBS (irritable bowel syndrome)	564.1
Influenza	487.1
Influenza, with pneumonia	487.0

Injection, tetanus	v03.7
Laryngitis, acute	464.00
Nausea	787.02
N & V	787.01
Pneumonia, acute	486
Pain, chest (precordial)	786.51
Pain, chest (midsternal)	786.51
Pain, chest (pressure)	786.59
Pain, joint	719.4
Pain, lower back (lumbago)	724.2
Pharyngitis (acute)	462
Sinusitis, acute	461.9
Sinusitis, acute maxillary	461.0
Strep throat	034.0
URI, acute	465.9
UTI	599.0

Locating an ICD-9-CM code

Critical Procedure Steps

1. Locate the patient's diagnosis.
2. Find the diagnosis in the Alphabetic Index.
3. Locate the code from the Alphabetic Index in the Tabular List.
4. Pick the most specific code available.
5. Record the code on the insurance claim form.

E codes

- Identify the external causes of injury or poisoning
- Always supplement a code that identifies the injury or condition
- Used in collecting public health information

V codes

- Identify encounters for reasons other than illness or injury
- May be used as a primary code or as an additional code

Tabular list organization

Chapter	Categories
1. Infectious and Parasitic Diseases	001–139
2. Neoplasms	140–239
3. Endocrine, Nutritional, and Metabolic Diseases, and Immunity Disorders	240–279
4. Diseases of the Blood and Blood-Forming Organs	280–289
5. Mental Disorders	290–319
6. Diseases of the Central Nervous System and Sense Organs	320–389
7. Diseases of the Circulatory System	390–459
8. Diseases of the Respiratory System	460–519

continued

Chapter	Categories
9. Diseases of the Digestive System	520–579
10. Diseases of the Genitourinary System	580–629
11. Complications of Pregnancy, Childbirth, and the Puerperium	630–679
12. Diseases of the Skin and Subcutaneous Tissue	680–709
13. Diseases of the Musculoskeletal System and Connective Tissue	710–739
14. Congenital Anomalies	740–759
15. Certain Conditions Originating in the Perinatal Period	760–779
16. Symptoms, Signs, and Ill-Defined Conditions	780–799
17. Injury and Poisoning	800–999

Supplementary Classifications

V Codes	V01–V83
E Codes	E800–E999

Procedural Coding

Add-on codes

These codes are used for procedures that are usually carried out in addition to another procedure.

Code modifiers

These modifiers show that some special circumstance applies to the service or procedure the physician performed.

Code ranges

Evaluation and Management	99201–99499
Anesthesiology	00100–01999
Surgery	10021–69990
Radiology	70010–79999
Pathology and Laboratory	80048–89356
Medicine	90281–99602

E and M codes

These codes help determine how to code differing levels of services. Guidelines determining level of service include:

- The extent of the patient history taken
- The extent of the exam conducted
- The complexity of the medical decision making
- Whether the patient is new or established

Locating a CPT code

Critical Procedure Steps

1. Check the patient's record for services performed.
2. Look up the procedure in the CPT index.
3. Determine appropriate modifiers.
4. Record the code on the insurance claim form.

Computer and Equipment Troubleshooting

Before calling a service agent:

- Check the simplest causes (power supply, equipment turned on, doors in appropriate position, etc.)
- Test the machine to see what it is failing to do
- Write down any error messages
- Check the equipment manual for a troubleshooting guide

Cultural Concerns

Communicating Effectively with Patients from Other Cultures and Meeting Their Needs for Privacy

Effective communication

1. When it is necessary to use a translator, direct the conversation or instruction to the translator.
2. Direct demonstrations to the patient of what to do, such as putting on an exam gown.
3. Confirm with the translator that the patient has understood the instruction or demonstration.
4. Allow the translator to be present during the exam if that is the patient's preference.
5. If the patient understands some English, speak slowly, use simple language, and demonstrate instructions whenever possible.

Meeting the need for privacy

1. Before the procedure, thoroughly explain to the patient or translator the reason for disrobing. Indicate that you will allow the patient privacy and ample time to undress.

2. If the patient is reluctant, reassure him that the physician respects the need for privacy and will look at only what is necessary for the exam.

3. Provide extra drapes if you think doing so will make the patient feel more comfortable.

4. If the patient is still reluctant, discuss the problem with the physician; the physician may be able to negotiate a compromise with the patient.

5. During the procedure, ensure that the patient is undraped only as much as necessary.

6. Whenever possible, minimize the amount of time the patient remains undraped.

Cultural Differences

YOU SHOULD KNOW

It is important that you understand the perceptions, behaviors, and expectations of people from different cultures. Keep in mind, patients from different cultural backgrounds may have differing beliefs about

- The cause of illness
- The presentation of symptoms and what they mean
- Treatment methods

Electronic Health Records (EHRs)

- Familiarize yourself with the program so that you may remain focused on the patient when entering data into the electronic health record
- When retrieving an EHR, make sure you have identified the patient with at least two identifiers, such as name, date of birth, and/or medical record number
- Keep your password information secure. Change the password often according to office policy
- Keep the computer that contains the EHRs secure and back up often
- Carefully check your entry before submitting—EHRs are legal documents

Filing Medical Records

Filing Steps

- **Inspecting**—prepare for filing
- **Indexing**—assign name or number to the file
- **Coding**—mark the file to identify it
- **Sorting**—alphabetically or numerically
- **Storing**—properly place the document or file

Filing Guidelines

- Be familiar with file contents
- Keep the file neat
- Do not crowd the folder or file drawer
- Position file guides 5 inches apart
- Cross-reference when appropriate

- File regularly
- Store files in their proper location
- Train personnel to file appropriately
- Periodically evaluate the filing system

Locating Misplaced Files

When searching for a misplaced file:

- Determine where the file was last seen
- Retrace your steps
- Check neighboring files in the cabinet
- Check underneath the cabinet for lost files
- Recheck the pile to be filed
- Check similar indexes
- Check with coworkers
- Check first name filing
- Look for files that stand out from others
- Determine if someone else could have picked up the file
- Have someone check behind you
- Straighten the office and check for lost file

Rules for Alphabetic Filing

Rules

1. Treat each part of a patient's name as a separate unit, and look at the units in this order: last name, first name, middle initial, and any subsequent names or initials.
2. Treat a prefix, such as the *O'* in *O'Hara,* as part of the name, not as a separate unit. Ignore variations in spacing, punctuation, and

capitalization. Treat prefixes such as *De La, Mac, Saint,* and *St.* exactly as they are spelled.

3. Treat hyphenated names as a single unit. Disregard the hyphen.

4. A title, such as *Dr.* or *Major,* or a seniority term, such as *Jr.* or *3d,* should be treated as the last filing unit to distinguish names that are otherwise identical.

Examples

- Stephen Jacobson

Unit 1	Unit 2	Unit 3	Unit 4
Jacobson	Stephen		

- Stephen Brent Jacobson

Unit 1	Unit 2	Unit 3	Unit 4
Jacobson	Stephen	Brent	

- Victor P. De La Cruz

Unit 1	Unit 2	Unit 3	Unit 4
Delacruz	Victor	P	

- Jean-Marie Vigneau

Unit 1	Unit 2	Unit 3	Unit 4
Vigneau	Jeanmarie		

- Dr. George B. Diaz

Unit 1	Unit 2	Unit 3	Unit 4
Diaz	George	B	Dr

- Major George B. Diaz

Unit 1	Unit 2	Unit 3	Unit 4
Diaz	George	B	Major

- James R. Foster, Jr.

Unit 1	Unit 2	Unit 3	Unit 4
Foster	James	R	Jr

Insurance Tips

Claims Process Overview

The general steps in the claims process include:

- Gathering and recording patient information
- Verifying the patient's insurance information
- Recording procedures and services
- Filing claims and billing patients
- Reviewing and recording payments

Completing a CMS-1500 Claim Form

Critical Procedure Steps

The numbers below correspond to the numbered fields on the CMS-1500 form. When completing the form, you should enter:

1. Insurance type

1a. Insured's insurance ID number

2. Patient's name (last, first, middle initial)

continued

3. Patient's birth date and sex
4. Insured's name or "same" if patient and insured are the same
5. Patient's mailing address
6. Patient's relationship to the insured
7. Insured's mailing address
8. Patient's marital, employment, and student status
9. Name of any other insuring party
9a. Policy number of other insuring party
9b. Date of birth and sex of other insured party
9c. Other insured's employer or school name
9d. Other insured's insurance plan
10. Information about the related cause of the condition
11. Insured's policy or group number
11a. Insured's date of birth and sex
11b. Employer's name or school name
11c. Insurance plan or program name
11d. Information about another insurance plan, if any
12. Patient or authorized representative signature and date
13. Insured's signature
14. Date of current illness, injury, or pregnancy
15. Nothing; leave blank for Medicare
16. Dates patient unable to work

17. Name of the referring physician, laboratory, or referring source

17a. UPIN

18. Dates the patient was hospitalized, if at all

19. Date the patient was last seen

20. Whether any laboratory tests were done at an outside lab

21. ICD-9-CM code or codes

22. Medicaid resubmission code and original reference number

23. Prior authorization number if required

24A. Date of service

24B. Place of service code

24C. Nothing; leave blank

24D. CPT/HCPCS codes

24E. Diagnosis code that applies to that procedure

24F. Fee charged

24G. Number of days or units on which the service is provided

24H. Medicaid specific information

24I. If service was in an emergency room

24J. Coordinated benefits

24K. Physician PIN

25. Federal tax ID number

26. Patient account number assigned by physician's office

continued

27. Assignment of benefits
28. Total charge
29. Amount already paid
30. Balance due
31. Physician signature and date
32. Name and address of service provider
33. Billing physician's name, address, and telephone number

Determining Primary Coverage

- If the patient has only one policy, it is primary.
- If the patient has two plans, the one that has been in effect the longest is primary.
- If the patient is also covered as a dependent on another plan, the patient's plan is primary.
- If an employed patient has coverage under the employer's plan and additional coverage under a government-sponsored plan, the employer's plan is primary.
- If a retired patient is covered by the plan of the spouse's employer and the spouse is still employed, the spouse's plan is primary.
- If a patient is a dependent child covered by both parent's plans and the parents are not separated or divorced, the primary plan is determined by which parent has the first birth date in the calendar year.
- If two or more plans cover the dependent children of separated or divorced parents who

do not have joint custody of their children, the children's primary plan is determined in this order:

- The plan of the custodial parent
- The plan of the spouse of the custodial parent (if the parent has remarried)
- The plan of the parent without custody

Elements of an EOB (Explanation of Benefits)

- Name and identification number of the insured
- Name of the beneficiary
- Claim number
- Date, place, and type of service
- Amount billed by the practice
- Amount allowed
- Amount of subscriber liability
- Amount paid and included in the current payment
- A notation of any services not covered and an explanation of why they were not covered

Generating Clean Claims

Insurance claims may be rejected because of missing info, including:

- Service facility name and complete address
- Medicare or benefits assignments indicator
- Referring provider name or indicator
- Subscriber's birth date
- Information about secondary insurance
- Payer name and/or payer identifier

Inventory

Inventory Procedures Overview

1. Define your role and responsibility in managing supplies.
2. Create a formal supply list of all administrative and clinical supplies.
3. Start a file containing a list of vendors and their current catalogs.
4. Create a want list of products.
5. Make a file for supply invoices and completed order forms.
6. Devise an inventory system for each item.
7. Devise a system for flagging items that need to be ordered or have already been ordered.
8. Establish a regular inventory schedule.
9. Order on a regular schedule unless an item is needed immediately.
10. Complete the vendor's order form.
11. Place the order by telephone, fax, e-mail, or online.
12. When the order arrives, check the shipment against the original order form and record the amount received on the individual inventory card or page.
13. Check the invoice and sign and date it when the order is received.
14. Write a check to the vendor according to office policy.
15. Mail the check to the vendor and file the invoice with the original order and the packing slip.

Recording Supply Inventory

You should devise an inventory system for each item used in a medical office. Keep a card or sheet for each item with the following information:

- Date and quantity of each order
- Name and contact information of the vendor and sales representative
- Date each shipment was received
- Total cost and unit cost for the item
- Payment method used
- Results of periodic counts of the item
- Quantity expected to cover the office for a given period of time
- Reorder quantity

Medical Records

Contents

- Patient registration form
- Patient medical history
- Physical exam results
- Results of laboratory and other tests
- Records from other physicians and hospitals
- Doctor's diagnosis and treatment plan
- Operative reports, follow-up visits, telephone calls
- Informed consent forms
- Hospital discharge summary forms
- Patient correspondence
- Faxed information

Making Corrections

Preparing the Record

Critical Procedure Steps

1. Create a chart label according to practice policy. The label may contain the patient's first and last name or a medical record number.
2. Appropriately place the label on the folder.
3. Appropriately place the date label on the folder, updating the date if necessary.
4. If alpha or numeric labels are used, place a patient name label according to office policy.
5. Punch holes in the appropriate forms for placement in the patient's chart.
6. Place all forms in the appropriate sections of the patient's chart.

Types of Medical Records

Problem-oriented medical record

- **Database**—patient's history, initial interview information, findings and results of physical exam, tests, x-rays, and other procedures
- **Problem list**—each patient problem is listed separately by number
- **Diagnostic and treatment plan**—laboratory and diagnostic tests and the physician's treatment plan
- **Progress notes**—notes on every condition or problem listed in the problem list

SOAP documentation

- *Subjective* data—the patient's description of his or her signs and symptoms
- *Objective* data—the physician's exam and test results
- *Assessment*—diagnosis or impression of a patient's diagnosis
- *Plan*—treatment options, chosen treatment, medications, tests, consultations, patient education, and follow-up

Releasing the Record

YOU SHOULD KNOW

- Obtain a signed and newly dated release from the patient authorizing the transfer of information.
- Make photocopies of the original material.

continued

29

- Send only those portions of the record covered by the release and only records originating from your facility.

- Do not send originals.

- Call the recipient to confirm that all materials were received.

Patient Bill of Rights

YOU SHOULD KNOW

Each patient has a right to:

- Receive considerate and respectful care

- Receive complete and current information concerning his or her diagnosis, treatment, and prognosis

- Know the identity of physicians, nurses, and others involved with his or her care as well as know when those involved are students, residents, or trainees

- Know the immediate and long-term costs of treatment choices

- Receive information necessary to give informed consent prior to the start of any procedure or treatment

- Have an advance directive concerning treatment or be able to choose a representative to make decisions

- Refuse treatment to the extent permitted by law

- Receive every consideration of his or her privacy
- Be assured of confidentiality
- Obtain reasonable responses to requests for services
- Obtain information about his or her health care, be allowed to review his or her medical record, and to have any information explained or interpreted
- Know whether treatment is experimental and be able to consent or decline to participate in proposed research studies or human experimentation
- Expect reasonable continuity of care
- Ask about and be informed of the existence of business relationships between the hospital and others that may influence the patient's treatment and care
- Know which hospital policies and practices relate to patient care, treatment, and responsibilities
- Be informed of available resources for resolving disputes, grievances, and conflicts, such as ethics committees or patient representatives
- Examine his or her bill and have it explained, and be informed of available payment methods

Patient Billing

Making a Bank Deposit

1. Divide bills, coins, checks, and money orders into separate piles.

2. Sort bills by denomination, total the amount, and record on the deposit slip on line market "Currency."

3. Put coins in wrappers or count and total then record on deposit slip on lined marked "Coin."

4. Review checks and money orders for proper endorsement.

5. List each check on the deposit slip, including the check number and amount.

6. List each money order on the deposit slip, including the notation MO and the writer's name.

7. Calculate the total deposit.

8. Record the total amount in the checkbook register.

9. Make the deposit in person or by mail.

10. Obtain a deposit receipt from the bank and file it for later use.

Patient History

Elements of a Patient History

- **Personal data**—name, patient number, birth date, etc.
- **Chief complaint**—the reason the patient is being seen
- **History of present illness**—information about the chief complaint including date of onset, what treatments the patient has done, and medications taken
- **Past medical history**—any and all health problems present and past
- **Family history**—health of the patient's family

- **Social and occupational history**—marital status, sexual behaviors and orientation, occupations, hobbies, use of chemical substances
- **Review of systems**—the physician completes a systematic review of each body system

Obtaining a Medical History

Critical Procedure Steps

1. Review the patient history form and plan your interview.
2. Bring the patient to a private room, identify yourself, and correctly identify the patient.
3. Explain the medical history form.
4. Ask appropriate questions using open-ended sentences.
5. Accurately document the patient's responses.
6. Offer to answer any questions.
7. Sign or initial the patient history form and file in the patient's chart.
8. Inform the physician that you have completed the medical history form.

Patient Interviewing Skills

- **Effective listening**—use active listening skills; provide feedback
- **Nonverbal clues and body language**—be aware of tone of voice, facial expression, and body language

- **Broad knowledge base**—stay abreast of new techniques, diseases, and symptoms
- **Summarizing**—when recording information, repeat back a summary of information to the patient

Patient Responsibilities

Each patient has a responsibility to:
- Provide information about past illnesses, hospitalizations, medications, and other matters related to her health status
- Participate in decision-making by asking for additional information about her health status or treatment when she does not fully understand information and instructions
- Provide health-care agencies with a copy of her written advance directive if she has one
- Inform physicians and other caregivers if she anticipates problems in following a prescribed treatment
- Follow the physician's orders for treatment
- Provide health-care agencies with necessary information for insurance claims and work with the health-care facility to make arrangements to pay fees when necessary

Payment Information Found in a Chart

Each patient chart should include the information necessary to file the patient's insurance and bill the patient for the remainder. When receiving a patient, make sure you review the chart for the following information:

- Address and phone number
- Insurance information
- Name of the person responsible for the payment

USPS State Abbreviations

Alabama AL	Maryland MD
Alaska AK	Massachusetts MA
Arizona AZ	Michigan MI
Arkansas AR	Minnesota MN
California CA	Mississippi MS
Colorado CO	Missouri MO
Connecticut CT	Montana MT
Delaware DE	Nebraska NE
District of Columbia DC	Nevada NV
Florida FL	New Hampshire NH
Georgia GA	New Jersey NJ
Hawaii HI	New Mexico NM
Idaho ID	New York NY
Illinois IL	North Carolina NC
Indiana IN	North Dakota ND
Iowa IA	Ohio OH
Kansas KS	Oklahoma OK
Kentucky KY	Oregon OR
Louisiana LA	Pennsylvania PA
Maine ME	Puerto Rico PR

Rhode Island RI

South Carolina SC

South Dakota SD

Tennessee TN

Texas TX

Utah UT

Vermont VT

Virginia VA

Washington WA

West Virginia WV

Wisconsin WI

Wyoming WY

2

Clinical

Ambulation

Crutch Gaits

Four point

1. Move the right crutch forward.
2. Move the left foot forward to the level of the left crutch.
3. Move the left crutch forward.
4. Move the right foot forward to level of the right crutch.

Three point

1. Move both crutches and the affected leg forward.
2. Move the unaffected leg forward while weight is balanced on both crutches.

Two point

1. Move the left crutch and the right foot forward at the same time.
2. Move the right crutch and the left foot forward at the same time.

Swing-to

1. Move both crutches forward at the same time.
2. Lift the body and swing to the crutches.
3. End with the tripod position again.

Swing-through

1. Move both crutches forward.
2. Move the body and swing past the crutches.

Teaching a Patient to Use Crutches

Patient Education Tips

1. Before educating the patient, verify the physician's order.
2. Explain the procedure to the patient.
3. Have the patient stand erect looking straight ahead.
4. Have the patient place the crutch tips 2 to 4 inches in front of and 4 to 6 inches to the side of each foot.
5. Ensure a 2-inch gap between the axilla and the axillary bar.
6. Teach the patient the get up from a chair.
7. Teach the patient the required gait.
8. Teach the patient to ascend stairs.
9. Teach the patient to descend stairs.

Using crutches: General guidelines

YOU SHOULD KNOW

- Do not lean on crutches
- Report any tingling or numbness in the arms, hands, or shoulders
- Support body weight with the hands
- Always stand erect to prevent muscle strain
- Look straight ahead when walking

- Move the crutches not more than 6 inches at a time to maintain good balance
- Check the crutch tips regularly for wear and replace as needed
- Check the crutch tips for wetness, dry the tips if they are wet
- Check all wing nuts and bolts for tightness
- Wear flat, well-fitting, nonskid shoes
- Remove throw rugs and other unsecured articles from traffic areas
- Report any unusual pain in the affected leg

Teaching a Patient to Use a Walker

Patient Education Tips
Walking

1. Instruct the patient to step into the walker.
2. Have the patient place her hands on the handgrips.
3. Make sure the patient's feet are far enough apart to provide a stable base.
4. Have the patient move the walker forward about 6 inches.
5. Instruct the patient to move one leg forward and then the other.
6. Instruct the patient to move the walker forward again to continue walking.

Patient Education Tips

Sitting

1. Have patient turn her back to the bed or chair.

2. Instruct the patient to take short, careful steps backward until she feels the bed or chair at the back of her legs.

3. Have the patient keep the walker in front of herself, let go of the walker, and place both hands on the bed or chair arms or seat.

4. Instruct the patient to balance herself on her arms while lowering herself slowly to the bed or chair.

Bandages

Circular

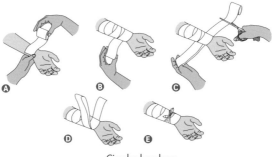

Circular bandage

Figure Eight

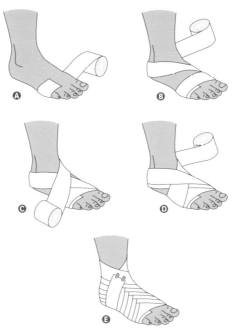

Figure eight bandage

Fingertip

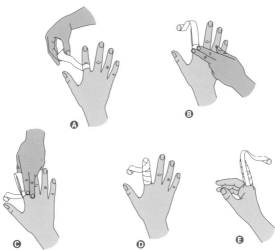

Fingertip bandage

Sling

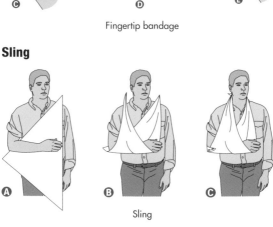

Sling

Triangular (Cravat)

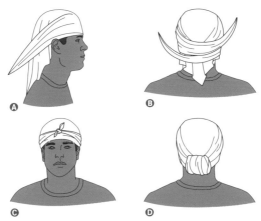

Cravat or triangular bandage

Biohazard Waste Disposal

Contaminated Paper Waste

Critical Procedure Steps

1. Wear gloves.
2. Dispose of contaminated waste in approved container.
3. When the container is full, secure the inner liner and place the entire container in the appropriate area for biohazardous waste.
4. Remove gloves and wash your hands.

Sharps

Critical Procedure Steps

1. Wear gloves.
2. Hold the object by blunt end.
3. Drop the object directly into the approved container.
4. Drop entire evacuation system into approved container.
5. Do not bend, break, or recap a needle.
6. Activate safety devices immediately after use.
7. Replace a container when it is two-thirds full.
8. Follow office procedure when disposing of containers.
9. Remove gloves and wash your hands.

Complimentary and Alternative Medicine

Common Therapies

Type of Therapy	Description
acupressure	The use of pressure, applied by hand, to various areas of the body in order to restore balance
acupuncture	A practice of inserting needles into various areas of the body to restore balance

Type of Therapy	Description
aromatherapy	The use of essential oils extracts or essences from flowers, herbs, and trees to promote health and well-being
Ayurveda	A system of medicine originating in India that uses herbal preparations, dietary changes, exercises, and meditation to restore health and promote well-being
biofeedback	A process in which an individual learns how to control involuntary body responses to promote health and treat disease
chiropractic medicine	Adjustments of the spine that are made to relieve pressure and/or pain
dietary supplements	Vitamins, minerals, herbals, and other substances taken by mouth without a prescription to promote health and well-being
homeopathy	A system of medicine that uses remedies in an attempt to stimulate the body to recover itself
hypnosis	A trance-like state usually induced by another person to access the subconscious mind and promote healing

continued

Type of Therapy	Description
magnetic therapy	A practice in which magnets are placed on the body to penetrate and correct the body's energy fields
massage	The use of pressure, kneading, stroking, and touch to alleviate pain and promote healing through relaxation
meditation	A state in which the body is consciously relaxed and the mind becomes calm and focused
naturopathy	A system of medicine that relies upon the healing power of the body and supports that power through various health-care practices such as nutrition, lifestyle, and exercise
reflexology	A manual therapy to the feet and/or hands in which pressure is applied to reflex "zones" mapped out on the feet and hands
Reiki	The use of visualization and touch to balance energy flow and bring healthy energy to affected body parts
therapeutic touch	The use of touch to detect and correct a person's energy fields, thus promoting healing and health

Type of Therapy	Description
traditional Chinese medicine (TCM)	Ancient system of medicine originating in China that involves preparations from herbal and animal sources to treat illness. This type of medicine includes various treatments such as acupuncture and acupressure
yoga	A series of poses and breathing exercises that provide awareness of the unity of a person's whole being (physical and spiritual)

Dietary Supplements

Herbals and other substances

1. Anabolic steroids
   - Uses/claims—promotes growth of skeletal muscles and the development of male sexual characteristics; used to improve sports performance
   - Side effects
     Men: reduced sperm production, shrinking of the testicles, male-pattern baldness, breast development
     Women: masculinization, breast size and body fat decrease, coarse skin, clitoris enlargement, deepened voice
   - Precautions/comments—can also cause short stature, heart enlargement or heart attacks, cancer, rage, mania, or delusions. Many side effects are irreversible. Addiction is possible. Withdrawal causes depression.

2. Black cohosh
   - Uses/claims—manages symptoms of menopause, such as hot flashes; lowers cholesterol
   - Side effects—stomach discomfort, headaches, heaviness in the legs, nausea, dizziness, increased perspiration, reduced pulse, visual disturbances
   - Precautions/comments—should not be taken by pregnant women or those with breast cancer

3. Cartilage (bovine and shark)
   - Uses/claims—treats cancer
   - Side effects—fatigue, nausea, fever, dizziness, bad taste in the mouth, scrotal swelling, constipation, vomiting, low blood pressure, cramping and/or bloating
   - Precautions/comments—can cause an abnormally high level of calcium in the blood

4. Coenzyme Q10
   - Uses/claims—treats cancer and Parkinson's disease
   - Side effects—mild insomnia, rash, nausea, fatigue
   - Precautions/comments—may interact with medications that lower cholesterol and blood sugar

5. Colloidal silver products
   - Uses/claims—treats infections and cancer
   - Side effects—argyria (bluish-gray color of skin because of excess silver), seizures, stomach distress, headaches, fevers, kidney damage, fatigue, and skin irritation

- Precautions/comments—may interfere with the absorption of penicillamine, quinolones, tetracyclines, and thyroxine
6. Cranberry
   - Uses/claims—relieves the symptoms of and reduces the risk of urinary tract infections
   - Side effects—diarrhea
   - Precautions/comments—excessive amounts may result in cramping and diarrhea
7. Echinacea
   - Uses/claims—aids in wound healing, stimulates immune function
   - Side effects—nausea, vomiting, unpleasant taste, abdominal pain, diarrhea
   - Precautions/comments—may shorten the duration of the common cold, may help prevent viral infection, although less effective
8. Essiac/Flor-Essence
   - Uses/claims—relieves pain, detoxify the body, strengthen the immune system, reduce tumor size
   - Side effects—nausea and vomiting, increased bowel movements, frequent urination, swollen glands, skin blemishes, flu-like symptoms, slight headaches
   - Precautions/comments—may increase tumor formation
9. Garlic
   - Uses/claims—lowers blood sugar and cholesterol levels, exhibits antiseptic and antibacterial activity

- Side effects—strong odor, burning of the mouth and esophagus, nausea, sweating, lightheadedness
- Precautions/comments—to be used cautiously by patients taking anticoagulant and/or antiplatelet agents, may interact with anticoagulant and/or antiplatelet agents

10. Ginger
   - Uses/claims—decreases nausea and vomiting, decreases cholesterol, stimulates circulation, decreases cough; used as flavoring; acts as a fungicide, pesticide
   - Side effects—high doses may cause drowsiness and decreased platelet aggregation
   - Precautions/comments—use caution in patients taking anticoagulant and/or antiplatelet agents.

11. Ginseng
   - Uses/claims—increases mental and physical capacity for work, relieves fatigue, enhances the immune system
   - Side effects—nervousness, agitation, breast nodules, vaginal bleeding, hypoglycemia
   - Precautions/comments—interacts with anticoagulants, loop diuretics, and antipsychotic drugs

12. Gingko
   - Uses/claims—increases circulation, improves memory, relieves anxiety or stress, alleviates tinnitus, improves the symptoms of asthma
   - Side effects—headache, dizziness, palpitations, rash, allergy, nausea, vomiting

- Precautions/comments—avoid in pregnancy and lactation, seeds contain toxin associated with seizures and death, discontinue 2 weeks prior to surgical or dental procedure to prevent increased bleeding

13. Glucosamine chondroitin
    - Uses/claims—treats osteoarthritis by reducing pain and slowing down joint cartilage damage
    - Side effects—elevated blood sugar
    - Precautions/comments—dosages vary greatly among manufacturers, glucosamine should be avoided in patients who are allergic to shellfish; diabetics and people using blood thinners should use with caution

14. Kava
    - Uses/claims—relieves the symptoms associated with stress; exhibits sedative activity
    - Side effects—skin rash, visual disturbances, risk of dependence
    - Precautions/comments—contraindicated in pregnancy, lactation, and patients who have depression; enhances the effect of other sedatives; not to be used while driving or operating heavy machinery; use should be limited to three months

15. Melatonin
    - Uses/claims—treats sleep disorders
    - Side effects—none noted with short-term use
    - Precautions/comments—long-term use is not suggested

16. Milk thistle
    - Uses/claims—protects the liver from damage and hepatitis C
    - Side effects—allergic reactions, stomach upset, nausea, diarrhea
    - Precautions/comments—none noted
17. Mistletoe extracts
    - Uses/claims—increases uterine and intestinal motility; provides anticancer activity
    - Side effects—allergy, toxic syndrome (nausea, delirium, bradycardia, hypertension, hallucinations, diarrhea)
    - Precautions/comments—all parts of the plant are toxic and may cause cardiac arrest
18. Methylsulfonal-methane (MSM)
    - Uses/claims—relieves stomach upset, improves immune system function, relieves musculoskeletal pain and arthritis
    - Side effects—none reported
    - Precautions/comments—possible vision problems
19. Omega-3 fatty acids
    - Uses/claims—improves heart health; reduces hypertension; improves rheumatoid arthritis, lupus, Raynaud's disease, and other autoimmune diseases, depression, prevent cancer
    - Side effects—possible fishy aftertaste, flatulence, diarrhea
    - Precautions/comments—intake is especially important in pregnancy; use with caution in patients who bruise or bleed easily or are taking heparin or warfarin

20. Reishi/Lingzhi
  - Uses/claims—improves immunity; anti-inflammatory; treats cancer, liver disease, AIDS, and high blood pressure
  - Side effects—dizziness, itchiness, and thirst resulting from increased defecation and urination
  - Precautions/comments—Reishi is the Japanese name and Lingzhi is the Chinese name; comes from the mushroom Ganoderma Lucidum
21. SAMe(S-adenosylmethionine)
  - Uses/claims—may enhance mood and help manage the symptoms of osteoarthritis, fibromyalgia, liver disorders, migraine headache, and insomnia
  - Side effects—nausea, vomiting
  - Precautions/comments—avoid use in patients with bipolar disorder, as the agent may trigger a manic phase
22. Saw palmetto
  - Uses/claims—relieves symptoms of benign prostatic hypertrophy
  - Side effects—nausea
  - Precautions/comments—contraindicated in pregnancy, may interfere with the metabolism of hormones
23. Soy
  - Uses/claims—prevents hot flashes and symptoms of menopause
  - Side effects—menstrual changes, stomach upset, diarrhea
  - Precautions/comments—use with caution in patients with thyroid conditions

24. St. John's Wort
   - Uses/claims—may enhance mood and have inhibitory effects on viruses
   - Side effects—dry mouth, dizziness, constipation, photosensitivity, confusion, insomnia, nervousness
   - Precautions/comments—products vary in content; avoid use with tricyclic antidepressants, selective serotonin reuptake inhibitors (SSRIs), and monoamine oxidase (MAO) inhibitors

25. Tea (green)
   - Uses/claims—lowers cholesterol levels; may decrease the risk of cancer; prevents cavities
   - Side effects—agitation, nervousness, insomnia, allergic reactions
   - Precautions/comments—use may impair iron metabolism, avoid use in individuals sensitive to caffeine

26. Valerian
   - Uses/claims—relieves insomnia
   - Side effects—drowsiness
   - Precautions/comments—avoid use with other sedative-hypnotic agents

Vitamins and minerals

1. Beta carotene
   - Megadose—more than 1.5 to 1.8 mg
   - Claims/benefits—improves the body's chemical reactions to dangerous free radicals, with health-promoting effects such as preventing lung cancer or heart disease for ex-smokers
   - Possible health hazard—lung cancer, death

2. Folic acid
   - Megadose—more than 1000 mg
   - Claims/benefits—reduces the risk of heart disease
   - Possible health hazard—no known adverse effects

3. Niacin
   - Megadose—slow-released doses of 500 mg or more or immediate-release doses of 750 mg or more
   - Claims/benefits—decreases cholesterol
   - Possible health hazard—stomach pain, vomiting, bloating, nausea, cramping, diarrhea, liver disease, muscle disease, eye damage, and heart injury

4. Selenium
   - Megadose—800 to 1000 micrograms
   - Claims/benefits—reduces cancer risk
   - Possible health hazard—tissue damage of the hair, nails, liver, nervous system, and teeth

5. Vitamin A
   - Megadose—25,000 or more international units
   - Claims/benefits—antioxidant that protects cells from free radicals that can cause chronic diseases
   - Possible health hazard—birth defects, bone abnormalities, and severe liver disease

6. Vitamin B$_6$
   - Megadose—more than 100 milligrams
   - Claims/benefits—treats asthma and cardio-vascular disease
   - Possible health hazard—balance difficulties, nerve injury causing changes in touch sensation

7. Vitamin C
   - Megadose—more than 100 mg
   - Claims/benefits—improves the body's chemical reactions to dangerous free radicals, with health-promoting effects such as preventing lung cancer or heart disease for ex-smokers
   - Possible health hazard—gastrointestinal distress and kidney stones
8. Vitamin D
   - Megadose—more than 2.5 mg
   - Claims/benefits—treats tuberculosis, rheumatoid arthritis, and skin disorders
   - Possible health hazard—bone demineralization, tendonitis, and skeletal pain, potential heart and kidney damage
9. Vitamin E
   - Megadose—more than 400 to 1000 international units
   - Claims/benefits—improves the body's chemical reactions to dangerous free radicals, with health-promoting effects such as preventing lung cancer or heart disease for ex-smokers.
   - Possible health hazard—increased blood coagulation, stroke, and death

Drug Interaction Examples

Dietary Supplements	Drug Type	Interaction
Garlic, gingko, ginger	Antiplatelet agents, anticoagulants	Increased risk of bleeding

Dietary Supplements	Drug Type	Interaction
St. John's Wort	Antidepressants	Increased blood pressure
Kava, valerian	Sedatives, benzodiazepines	Increased sedative effects
Ginseng	Decongestants, sympathomimetics	Increased nervousness, insomnia, agitation, palpitations

Source: Reprinted courtesy of the Food and Drug Administration.

Drug Abuse

Symptoms Associated with Abused Drugs

Drug Names/Type	Symptoms, Effects
Amphetamines/ stimulants	Altered mental status, from confusion to paranoia; hyperactivity, then exhaustion; insomnia; loss of appetite
Anabolic steroids	Irritability, aggression, nervousness, male-pattern baldness
Barbiturates/sedatives	Slowed thinking, slowed reflexes, slowed respiration, loss of anxiety

continued

Drug Names/Type	Symptoms, Effects
Benzodiazepines/ sedatives	Poor coordination, drowsiness, increased self-confidence
Cocaine/stimulant	Alternating euphoria and apprehension, intense craving for more of the drug
Ecstasy/psychoactive	Confusion, depression, anxiety, paranoia, increased heart rate and blood pressure
GHB/depressants	Slow pulse and breathing, lowered blood pressure, drowsiness, poor concentration
Inhalants	Stimulation, intoxication, hearing loss, arm or leg spasms
LSD/hallucinogen	Heightened sense of awareness, grandiose hallucinations, mystical experiences, flashbacks
Marijuana, cannabinoids, Hashish	Altered thought processes, distorted sense of time and self, impaired short-term memory
Opium, morphine, codeine/opiate narcotics	Decreased level of consciousness, detachment, drowsiness, impaired judgment
PCP/hallucinogen	Decreased awareness of surroundings, hallucinations, poor perception of time and distance, possible overdose and death

Ear Irrigation

Critical Procedure Steps

1. Identify the patient and explain the procedure.
2. Check the order.
3. Compare the solution with the order three times.
4. Wash your hands and put on gloves, a gown, and a face shield.
5. Look in the patient's ear to identify if cerumen or a foreign body needs to be removed.
6. Assemble the supplies.
7. Warm the solution to room temperature.
8. Have the patient sit or lie down with the affected ear facing you.
9. Place a towel over the patient's shoulder and have her hold the basin under her ear.
10. Pour the solution into another basin.
11. If necessary, gently clean the patient's outer ear.
12. Fill the irrigating syringe with the solution.
13. Straighten the ear canal by pulling upward and outward for adults or down and back for infants and children.

continued

14. Holding the tip of the syringe ½ inch from the ear canal, slowly instill the solution into the ear.

15. Refill the syringe and continue irrigation until the canal is cleaned or the solution is used up.

16. Dry the external ear with a cotton ball, and leave a clean cotton ball loosely in place for 5 to 10 minutes.

17. If the patient becomes dizzy, allow her time to regain balance before standing.

18. Properly dispose of used disposable supplies.

19. Remove your gloves, gown, and face shield, and wash your hands.

20. Record in the patient's chart the procedure and result, the amount of solution used, the time of administration, and the ear(s) irrigated.

21. Put on gloves and clean the equipment and room according to OSHA guidelines.

ECGs

Artifacts

AC interference

- Cause: The electrocardiograph picks up small amounts of electric current given off by other pieces of equipment in the room.
- Example:

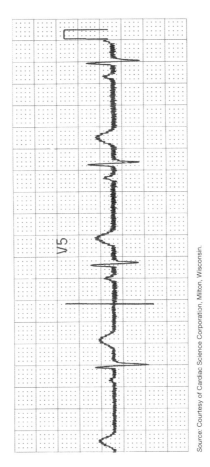

Source: Courtesy of Cardiac Science Corporation, Milton, Wisconsin.

V5

- Solution: Turn off or unplug other appliances in the room.

Flat line

- Cause: There may be a loose or discon-
  nected wire or two of the wires may have been
  switched. A flat line may indicate cardiac arrest.

- Example:

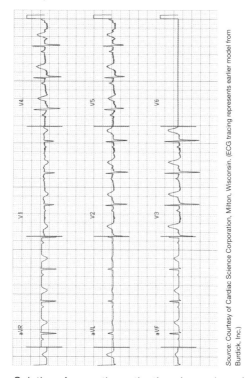

Source: Courtesy of Cardiac Science Corporation, Milton, Wisconsin. (ECG tracing represents earlier model from Burdick, Inc.)

- Solution: Assess the patient's pulse and respirations first, then check all lead connections.

Somatic interference

- Cause: Muscle movement
- Example:

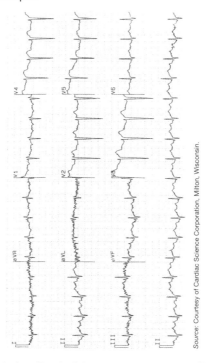

- Solution: Remind the patient to remain still and refrain from talking. If the patient is cold, offer him a blanket. If the patient is unable to stop a tremor, place the limb electrodes closer to the trunk of the body.

Wandering baseline

- Causes: Somatic interference, mechanical problems, and improper electrode application
- Example:

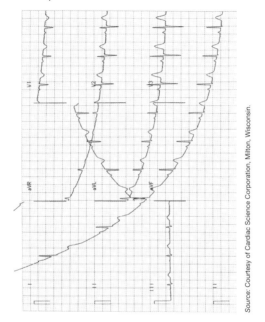

Source: Courtesy of Cardiac Science Corporation, Milton, Wisconsin.

- Solution: Remind the patient to remain still, clean any oil or lotions from the skin before applying electrodes, check the electrodes and reapply if necessary, uncross any crossed wires, and reposition any dangling wires.

Critical Arrhythmias

When performing an ECG, recognizing critical arrhythmias is essential. The following pages illustrate atrial fibrillation, premature ventricular contractions, and ventricular fibrillation.

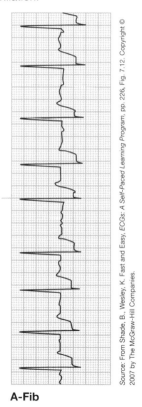

Source: From Shade, B., Wesley, K. Fast and Easy, *ECGs: A Self-Paced Learning Program,* pp. 226, Fig. 7.12. Copyright © 2007 by The McGraw-Hill Companies.

A-Fib

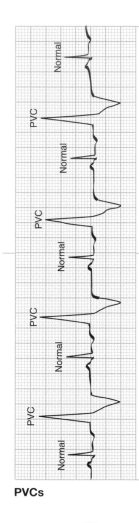

PVCs

Source: From Shade, B., Wesley, K. *Fast and Easy, ECGs: A Self-Paced Learning Program*, pp. 333, Fig. 11.6a. Copyright © 2007 by The McGraw-Hill Companies.

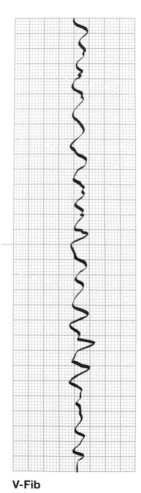

V-Fib

Source: From Shade, B., Wesley, K. Fast and Easy, *ECGs: A Self-Paced Learning Program,* pp. 344, Fig. 11.17. Copyright © 2007 by The McGraw-Hill Companies.

Lead Placement

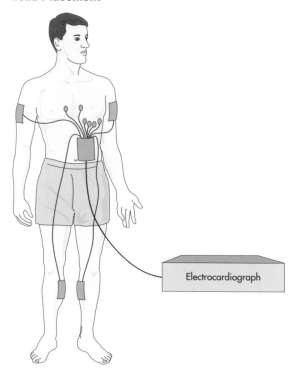

Electrocardiograph

Parts of the ECG

P wave

- Appearance—small upward curve
- Represents SA node impulse, wave of depolarization through the atria, and resultant contraction

QRS complex

- Appearance—includes Q, R, and S waves
- Represents—contraction of the ventricles; the QRS complex is larger than the P wave because the ventricles are larger than the atria

Q wave

- Appearance—downward deflection
- Represents—an impulse traveling down the septum toward the Purkinje fibers

R wave

- Appearance—large upward spike
- Represents—an impulse going through the left ventricle

S wave

- Appearance—downward deflection
- Represents—an impulse going through both ventricles

T wave

- Appearance—upward curve
- Represents—recovery of the ventricles

U wave

- Appearance—small upward curve sometimes found after the T wave
- Represents—may be seen in normal individuals, in patients who experience slow recovery of Purkinje fibers, or in patients who have low potassium levels or other metabolic disturbances

P-R interval

- Appearance—includes the P wave and the straight line connecting it to the QRS complex
- Represents—the time it takes for electrical impulse to travel from the SA node to the AV node

Q-T interval

- Appearance—includes QRS complex, S-T segment, and T wave
- Represents—the time it takes for the ventricles to contract and recover

S-T segment

- Appearance—connects the end of the QRS complex with the beginning of the T wave
- Represents—the time between contraction of ventricles and recovery

Emergencies

Assisting in a Disaster

Type of Disaster	Action to Take
Weather disaster, such as a flood or hurricane	• Report to the community command post. • Have your credentials with you. • Receive an identifying tag or vest and assignment.

Type of Disaster	Action to Take
	• Accept only an assignment that is appropriate for your abilities. Expect to be part of a team.
	• Document what medical care each victim receives on each person's disaster tag.
Office fire	• Activate the alarm system.
	• Use a fire extinguisher if the fire is confined to a small container, such as a trash can.
	• Turn off oxygen.
	• Shut windows and doors.
	• Seal doors with wet cloths to prevent smoke from entering.
	• If evacuation is necessary, proceed quietly and calmly. Direct ambulatory patients and family members to the appropriate exit route. Assist patients who need help leaving the building.

Assisting with an Emergency Childbirth

Critical Procedure Steps

1. Ask the woman her name and age, how far apart her contractions are (about two per minute signals that the birth is near), if her

continued

water has broken, and if she feels straining or pressure as if the baby is coming. Alert the doctor or call the EMS system.

2. Help remove the woman's lower clothing.

3. Explain that you are about to do a visual inspection to see if the baby's head is in position. Ask the woman to lie on her back with her thighs spread, her knees flexed, and her feet flat. Examine her to see if there is crowning.

4. If the head is crowning, childbirth is imminent. Place clean cloths under the woman's buttocks, and use sterile sheets or towels (if they are available) to cover her legs and stomach.

5. Wash your hands thoroughly and put on exam gloves. If other PPE is available, put it on now.

6. At this point the physician would begin to take steps to deliver the baby, and you would position yourself at the woman's head to provide emotional support and help in case she vomited. If no physician is available, position yourself at the woman's side so that you have a constant view of the vaginal opening.

7. Talk to the woman and encourage her to relax between contractions while allowing the delivery to proceed naturally.

8. Position your gloved hands at the woman's vaginal opening when the baby's head starts to appear. Do not touch her skin.

9. Place one hand below the baby's head as it is delivered. Spread your fingers evenly around the baby's head.

   Use your other hand to help cradle the baby's head. Never pull on the baby.

10. If the umbilical cord is wrapped around the baby's neck, gently loosen the cord and slide it over the baby's head.

11. If the amniotic sac has not broken by the time the baby's head is delivered, use your finger to puncture the membrane. Then pull the membranes away from the baby's mouth and nose.

12. Wipe blood or mucus from the baby's mouth with a clean cloth.

13. Continue to support the baby's head as the shoulders emerge. The upper shoulder will deliver first, followed quickly by the lower shoulder.

14. After the feet are delivered, lay the baby on his side with the head slightly lower than the body. Keep the baby at the same level as the mother until you cut the umbilical cord.

15. If the baby is not breathing, lower the head, raise the lower part of the body, and tap the soles of the feet. If the baby is still not breathing, begin rescue breathing and CPR.

continued

16. To cut the cord, wait several minutes, until pulsations stop. Use the clamps or pieces of string to tie the cord in two places.

17. Use sterilized scissors to cut the cord in between the placement of the two clamps or pieces of string.

18. Within 10 minutes of the baby's birth, the placenta will begin to expel. Save it in a plastic bag for further examination.

19. Keep the mother and baby warm by wrapping them in towels or blankets. Do not touch the baby any more than necessary.

20. Massage the mother's abdomen just below the navel every few minutes to control internal bleeding.

21. Arrange for transport of the mother and baby to the hospital.

Calling Poison Control

Information you will need to know:

- The patient's age
- The name of the poison
- The amount of poison swallowed
- When the poison was swallowed
- Whether or not the person has vomited
- How long it will take to get the patient to a medical facility

Caring for a Patient Who Is Vomiting

Critical Procedure Steps

1. Wash your hands and put on exam gloves and other PPE.

2. Ask the patient when and how the vomiting started and how frequently it occurs. Find out whether she is nauseated or in pain.

3. Give the patient an emesis basin to collect vomit. Observe and document its amount, color, odor, and consistency. Particularly note blood, bile, undigested food, or feces in the vomit.

4. Place a cool compress on the patient's forehead to make her more comfortable. Offer water and paper tissues or a towel to clean her mouth.

5. Monitor for signs of dehydration, such as confusion, irritability, and flushed, dry skin. Also monitor for signs of electrolyte imbalances, such as leg cramps or an irregular pulse.

6. If requested, assist by laying out supplies and equipment for the physician to use in administering intravenous fluids and electrolytes. Administer an antinausea drug if prescribed.

7. Prepare the patient for diagnostic tests if instructed.

8. Remove the gloves and wash your hands.

Cast Care

- Report any of the following to the physician immediately: pain, swelling, discoloration of exposed portions, lack of pulsation and warmth, or the inability to move exposed parts.
- Keep the casted extremity elevated for the first day.
- Avoid indenting the cast until it is completely dry.
- Check the movement and sensation of the visible extremities frequently.
- Restrict strenuous activities for the first few days.
- Avoid allowing the affected limb to hang down for any length of time.
- Do not put anything inside the cast.
- Keep the cast dry.
- Follow the physician's orders about restricting activities.

Choosing PPE During an Emergency

Equipment	Conditions for Use
Gloves	Chance of contact with blood or other body secretion or excretion during emergency
Goggles and mask or face shield and possible head cover	Chance of blood or other body secretion or excretion being splattered, coughed, or sprayed onto the mucus membranes of the eyes, mouth, or nose

Equipment	Conditions for Use
Gown and possible booties	Chance of contact with excessive bleeding or secretion and excretion
Pocket mask or mouth shield	Needed for CPR or rescue breathing

Cleaning Minor Wounds

Critical Procedure Steps

1. Wash your hands and put on gloves.
2. Dip gauze squares in warm soapy water.
3. Wash the wound from the center outward.
4. Remove debris as you wash.
5. Rinse the wound.
6. Pat the wound dry with sterile gauze.
7. Cover the wound with a dry, sterile dressing.
8. Bandage the dressing in place.
9. Properly dispose of contaminated materials.
10. Remove gloves and wash your hands.
11. Instruct the patient on wound care.
12. Document the procedure in the patient's chart.

Concussion

Patient Education Tips

After a concussion, teach patients the following guidelines:

- Inform the patient that the first 24 hours after the injury are the most critical.

- Tell the patient to refrain from strenuous activity, to rest, and to return to regular activity gradually. Instruct the patient to avoid using pain medicines other than acetaminophen, unless the drugs are approved by the physician.

- Advise the patient to eat lightly, especially if nausea and vomiting occur.

- Tell a family member to check on the patient every few hours. The family member should make sure the patient knows his own name, his location, and the name of the family member.

- Instruct the family member to call for medical assistance immediately if the patient exhibits any of these warning signs:
  - Any symptom that is getting worse, such as headaches, sleepiness, or nausea, including nausea that doesn't go away
  - Changes in behavior, such as irritability or confusion
  - Dilated pupils (pupils that are bigger than normal) or pupils of different sizes
  - Trouble walking or speaking
  - Drainage of bloody or clear fluids from ears or nose
  - Vomiting

- **S**eizures
- **W**eakness or numbness in the arms or legs
- **A** less serious head injury in a patient taking blood thinners or who has a bleeding disorder such as hemophilia

Controlling Bleeding

Critical Procedure Steps

1. If you have time, wash your hands and put on exam gloves, face protection, and a gown.

2. Using a clean or sterile dressing, apply direct pressure over the wound.

3. If blood soaks through the dressing, do not remove it. Apply an additional dressing over the original one.

4. If possible, elevate the body part that is bleeding.

5. If direct pressure and elevation do not stop the bleeding, apply pressure over the nearest pressure point between the bleeding and the heart. For example, if the wound is on the lower arm, apply pressure on the brachial artery. For a lower-leg wound, apply pressure on the femoral artery in the groin.

6. When the doctor or EMT arrives, assist as requested.

7. After the patient has been transferred to a hospital, properly dispose of contaminated materials.

continued

8. Remove the gloves and wash your hands.

9. Document your care in the patient's chart.

Estimating the Extent of a Burn

Use these charts to calculate the percentage of body surface affected by burns.

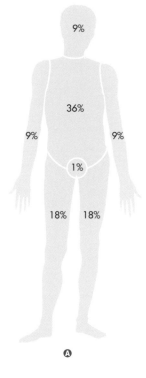

Ⓐ

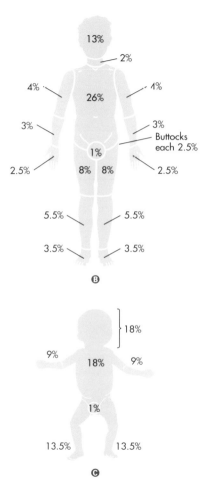

13%

2%

4% 1%

26%

3% 3%

Buttocks
each 2.5%

2.5% 2.5%

1%

8% 8%

5.5% 5.5%

3.5% 3.5%

Ⓑ

18%

9% 9%

18%

1%

13.5% 13.5%

Ⓒ

Fractures, Dislocations, Sprains, and Strains

Basic emergency steps

- Keep the person calm and limit his movement.
- Assess him for any other injuries.
- Notify the doctor or call EMS. Do not move the patient until the doctor or EMS arrives.
- If the skin is broken, cover with a sterile dressing.
- Immobilize the extremity with a splint or sling. Use rolled-up newspaper, strips of wood, etc. to immobilize above and below the injury.
- Do not try to put the bone back into place. Immobilize it in the position it was found.
- Place an icepack on the affected area.
- Monitor him for signs of shock.
- Assess for signs of lack of circulation.

Performing an Emergency Assessment

Critical Procedure Steps

1. Put on gloves.
2. Form a general impression of the patient.
3. Gather information from the patient or bystanders about the incident.
4. Assess an unresponsive patient by tapping her shoulder and asking "Are you OK?"
5. Assess the patient's airway.
6. Assess the patient's circulation.
7. Perform a head-to-toe focused exam.

8. Recheck vital signs and assess for signs of shock.

9. Report your findings to the doctor or EMS.

10. Document your findings in the patient chart.

11. Assist the doctor or EMS as requested.

12. Dispose of hazardous waste as required.

13. Remove your gloves and wash your hands.

Performing Triage in a Disaster

Critical Procedure Steps

1. Wash your hands and put on exam gloves and other PPE if available.

2. Quickly assess each victim.

3. Sort victims by type of injury and need for care, classifying them as emergent, urgent, nonurgent, or dead.

4. Label the emergent patients no. 1, and send them to appropriate treatment stations immediately. Emergent patients, such as those who are in shock or who are hemorrhaging, need immediate care.

5. Label the urgent patients no. 2, and send them to basic first-aid stations. Urgent patients need care within the next several hours. Such patients may have lacerations that can be dressed quickly to stop the bleeding but can wait for suturing.

continued

6. Label nonurgent patients no. 3, and send them to volunteers who will be empathic and provide refreshments. Nonurgent patients are those for whom timing of treatment is not critical, such as patients who have no physical injuries but who are emotionally upset.

7. Label patients who are dead no. 4. Ensure that the bodies are moved to an area where they will be safe until they can be identified and proper action can be taken.

Eye Irrigation

Critical Procedure Steps

1. Identify the patient and explain the procedure.

2. Review the order.

3. Compare the solution with the order three times.

4. Wash your hands and put on gloves, a gown, and a face shield.

5. Assemble the supplies.

6. Ask the patient to lie down or sit with his head tilted back and to the side that is being irrigated.

7. Place a towel over the patient's shoulder and have the patient hold the basin under the eye that is being irrigated.

8. Pour the solution into another basin.

9. Fill the irrigating syringe with solution.

10. Hold a tissue on the patient's cheekbone with your nondominant hand, and press down to expose the patient's eye socket.
11. Holding the tip of the syringe ½ inch from the eye, direct the solution onto the patient's conjunctiva from the inside to the outside.
12. Do not allow the solution to enter the other eye.
13. Do not direct the solution towards the cornea.
14. Do not use excessive force.
15. Refill the syringe and continue the irrigation until the prescribed amount of solution is used.
16. Dry the area around the eye with tissues.
17. Properly dispose of disposable supplies.
18. Remove your gloves, gown, and face shield, and wash your hands.
19. Record in the patient's chart the procedure, the amount of solution used, the time of administration, and the eye(s) irrigated.
20. Put on gloves and clean the equipment and room according to OSHA guidelines.

Gynecology

Assisting with a Gynecology Exam

Critical Procedure Steps

1. Gather equipment and make sure all items are in working order. Correctly label the slide and/or the collection vials.

continued

2. Identify the patient and explain the procedure.

3. Have the patient remove all clothing, including underwear, and put the gown on with the opening in the front.

4. Ask the patient to sit on the edge of the examining table with the drape until the physician arrives.

5. When the physician is ready, have the patient place her feet into the stirrups and move her buttocks to the edge of the table.

6. Provide the physician with gloves and an exam lamp as she examines the genitalia by inspection and palpation.

7. Pass the speculum to the physician. To increase patient comfort, you may place it in warm water before handing it to the physician. Do not use a water-based lubricant.

8. For the Pap (Papanicolaou) smear, be prepared to pass a cotton-tipped applicator and cervical brush, broom, or scraper for the collection of the specimens.

9. Have the labeled slide or vial available for the physician.

10. Once the specimen is on the slide, a cytology fixative must be applied immediately. A spray fixative is common, and it should be held 6 inches from the slide and sprayed

lightly with a back and forth motion. Allow the slide to dry completely.

11. Cells collected for thin-layer preparation should be washed into the collection vial.

12. After the physician removes the speculum, provide the physician with additional lubricant as needed for the digital exam.

13. Upon completion of the exam, help the patient into a supine or sitting position.

14. Provide tissues or moist wipes for the patient to remove the lubricant, and ask the patient to get dressed.

15. Explain the procedure for communicating the laboratory results.

16. After the patient has left, don gloves and clean the exam room and equipment.

17. Dispose of the disposable speculum, specimen collection devices, and other contaminated waste in a biohazardous waste container.

18. Store the supplies, straighten the room, and discard the used exam paper on the table.

19. Prepare the laboratory requisition slip, and place it and the specimen in the proper place for transport to an outside laboratory.

20. Remove your gloves and wash your hands.

Assisting with a Cervical Biopsy

Critical Procedure Steps

1. Identify the patient and introduce yourself.

2. Look at the patient's chart, and ask the patient to confirm information or explain any changes. Specific patient information you need to ask about and note in the chart includes the following:
   - Date of birth and Social Security number (verify that you have the correct chart for the correct patient)
   - Date of last menstrual period
   - Method of contraception, if any
   - Previous gynecologic surgery
   - Use of hormone replacement therapy or other steroids

3. Describe the biopsy procedure to the patient, noting that a piece of tissue will be removed to diagnose the cause of her problem. Explain that it may be painful but only for the brief moment during which tissue is taken.

4. Give the patient a gown, if needed, and a drape. Direct her to undress from the waist down and to wrap the drape around herself. Tell her to sit at the end of the examining table.

5. Wash your hands and put on exam gloves.

6. Using sterile method, open the sterile pack to create a sterile field on the tray or Mayo

stand, and arrange the instruments with transfer forceps. Add the vaginal speculum and sterile supplies to the sterile field.

7. When the physician arrives in the examining room, ask the patient to lie back, place her heels in the stirrups of the table, and move her buttocks to the edge of the table.

8. Assist the physician by arranging the drape so that only the genitalia are exposed, and place the light so that the genitalia are illuminated.

9. Use transfer forceps to hand instruments and supplies to the physician as he requests them. You may don sterile gloves and hand the physician supplies and instruments directly. When he is ready to obtain the biopsy, tell the patient that it may hurt. If she seems particularly fearful, instruct her to take a deep breath and let it out slowly.

10. When the physician hands you the instrument with the tissue specimen, place the specimen in the specimen container and discard the instrument in the appropriate container.

11. Label the specimen container with the patient's name, the date and time, cervical or endocervical (as indicated by the physician), the physician's name, and your initials.

12. Place the container and the cytology laboratory requisition form in the envelope or bag provided by the laboratory.

continued

13. When the physician has removed the vaginal speculum, place it in the clean basin for later sanitization, disinfection, and sterilization. Properly dispose of used supplies and disposable instruments.

14. Remove the gloves and wash your hands.

15. Tell the patient that she may get dressed. Inform her that she may have some vaginal bleeding for a couple of days, and provide her with a sanitary napkin. Instruct her not to take tub baths or have intercourse and not to use tampons for 2 days. Encourage her to call the office if she experiences problems or has questions.

Cervical Specimen Collection and Submission Guidelines

YOU SHOULD KNOW

In order to ensure that the cervical specimen collected is adequate for optimal screening, the American Society of Cytopathology has certain clinical guidelines. As a medical assistant, you will be responsible for helping the physician implement these guidelines. These include:

Collecting patient information:

- Scheduling a patient appointment about two weeks after the patient's last menstrual period
- Instructing patients not to douche, use tampons, foams, or jellies, or have sexual intercourse 48 hours prior to the test

- Completing a Lab Requisition Form, which includes the following information:
  - Patient name (note any recent name changes)
  - Date of birth
  - Menstrual status (last menstrual period, hysterectomy, etc.)
  - Any patient risk factors
  - Specimen source

Completing a specimen label:

- Glass slide
  - Label the frosted end of the slide with the patient's first and last name
  - Include additional identifier, such as the patient record number.
- Liquid samples
  - Complete all requested information on label and affix to vial.

Meeting the Needs of the Pregnant Patient During an Exam

Critical Procedure Steps

Providing Patient Information

1. Identify the patient and introduce yourself.

2. Assess the patient's need for education by asking appropriate questions.

3. Provide any appropriate instructions or materials.

continued

4. Ask the patient whether she has any special concerns or questions about her pregnancy that she might want to discuss with the physician.

5. Communicate the patient's concerns or questions to the physician; include all pertinent background information on the patient.

Ensuring Comfort During the Exam

1. Identify the patient and introduce yourself.

2. Wash your hands.

3. Explain the procedure to the patient.

4. Provide a gown or drape, and instruct the patient in the proper way to wear it after disrobing. (Allow the patient privacy while disrobing, and assist only if she requests help.)

5. Ask the patient to step on the stool or the pullout step of the examining table.

6. Assist the patient onto the examining table.

7. Keeping position restrictions in mind, help the patient into the position requested by the physician.

8. Provide and adjust additional drapes as needed.

9. Keep in mind any difficulties the patient may have in achieving a certain position; suggest alternative positions whenever possible.

10. Minimize the time the patient must spend in uncomfortable positions.

11. If the patient appears to be uncomfortable during the procedure, ask whether she would like to reposition herself or take a break; assist as necessary.

12. To prevent pelvic pooling of blood and subsequent dizziness or hyperventilation, allow the patient time to adjust to sitting before standing after she has been lying on the examining table.

Pap Smear Classifications

The Bethesda System

Classification	What It Means
Negative • ASC-US—atypical squamous cells of undetermined significance • ASC-H—atypical squamous cells that cannot exclude a high-grade squamous intraepithelial lesion	No intraepithelial lesion or malignancy • ASC-US—Considered a mild abnormality; may be related to HPV infection • ASC-H—May be at risk of being precancerous
AGC—atypical glandular cells	Glandular cells do not appear normal, but it is uncertain what the changes mean

continued

Classification	What It Means
AIS—endocervical adenocarcinoma in situ	Precancerous cells are found in the glandular tissue
LSIL—low-grade squamous intraepithelial lesion	Early changes in cells and an area of abnormal tissue; mild abnormalities caused by HPV infection
HSIL—high-grade squamous intraepithelial lesion	Marked changes in the size and shape of the abnormal cells; a higher likelihood of progressing to invasive cancer

Heat and Cold Therapy Guidelines

Administering Cryotherapy

Critical Procedure Steps

1. Check the physician's order for location and length of time of therapy.
2. Identify the patient and explain the procedure.
3. Have the patient undress and put on a gown if required.
4. Wash your hands and put on gloves.
5. Position the patient comfortably and drape appropriately.
6. Prepare the therapy as ordered.

7. Place the device on the patient's affected body part.

8. Ask the patient how the device feels.

9. Leave in place for the ordered amount of time (no longer than 20 minutes).

10. Remove the application and observe the area for reduced swelling, redness, and pain.

11. If the patient has a dressing, replace it.

12. Assist the patient as necessary.

13. Remove any equipment and supplies and properly dispose of biohazardous waste.

14. Remove your gloves and wash your hands.

15. Document the treatment and your observations in the patient chart.

Administering Thermotherapy

Critical Procedure Steps

1. Check the physician's order for location and length of time of therapy.

2. Identify the patient and explain the procedure.

3. Have the patient undress and put on a gown if required.

4. Wash your hands and put on gloves.

continued

5. Position the patient comfortably and drape appropriately.

6. If the patient has a dressing, check the dressing for blood and change if necessary.

7. Prepare the therapy as ordered.

8. Check the temperature by feel and assess the patient for signs of adverse skin conditions.

9. Place the device on the patient's affected body part.

10. Ask the patient how the device feels.

11. Leave in place for the ordered amount of time.

12. Check periodically for signs of adverse skin conditions.

13. Remove the application and observe the area.

14. Replace the patient's dressing if indicated.

15. Help the patient dress, if necessary.

16. Remove any equipment and supplies and properly dispose of biohazardous waste.

17. Remove your gloves and wash your hands.

18. Document the treatment and your observations in the patient chart.

Contraindications to Heat and Cold Therapy

Therapy	Contraindications
Dry and moist cold applications	Severe circulatory problems, inability to tolerate weight of device, pain caused by application (more common with moist cold)
Dry and moist hot applications	Possibility of hemorrhage, malignancy; acute inflammation, such as appendicitis; severe circulation problems; pain caused by weight of device

Holter Monitor

Holter Monitoring

Critical Procedure Steps

1. Have patient remove clothing from the waist up.
2. Place the patient in a comfortable position.
3. Prepare the patient's skin at the electrode sites.
4. Apply the electrodes.
5. Attach the wires to the electrodes.
6. Attach the patient cable.

continued

7. Insert a fresh battery, and position the unit.

8. Tape wires, cable, and electrodes as necessary.

9. Insert cassette tape and turn on the unit.

10. Confirm that the tape is running and note the start time in the patient's chart.

11. Instruct the patient on proper use of the monitor and how to make entries in the diary.

12. Schedule the patient's return visit.

Patient Education Tips

Before Holter monitoring, instruct the patient to:

- **C**ontinue normal activities during Holter monitoring.
- **R**ecord all activities, emotional upsets, physical symptoms, and medications taken.
- **W**ear loose-fitting clothing that opens in the front.
- **A**void magnets, metal detectors, high-voltage areas, and electric blankets during the monitoring period.
- **A**void getting the monitor wet.
- **C**heck the monitor to make sure it is working.

Immunization Schedule

Adolescent

General recommendations for ages 7 to 18 years:

Age in Years ▶ Vaccine ▼	7–10	11–12	13–14	15–16	17–18
Tdap		☑			
HPV		☑			
Meningococcal		☑		☑	
Pneumococcal	For certain high-risk groups				
Influenza	Yearly for high-risk groups				
Hepatitis A	Series for high-risk groups				
Hepatitis B	Catch-up vaccinations only				
IPV	Catch-up vaccinations only				
MMR	Catch-up vaccinations only				
Varicella	Catch-up vaccinations only				

Adult

General recommendations for adults:

Age in Years ▶ Vaccine ▼	19–49	50–64	≥65
Td/Tdap	Every 10 years		
HPV	3 doses, females		

continued

Age in Years ▶ Vaccine ▼	19–49	50–64	≥65
MMR	1 or 2 doses	1 dose for high-risk pts.	
Varicella	2 doses		
Influenza	Annually for high-risk patients	Annually	
Pneumococcal	1-2 doses for high-risk patients		1 dose
Hepatitis A	2 doses for high-risk pts.		
Hepatitis B	3 doses for high-risk pts.		
Meningococcal	1 dose for high-risk pts.		

Child

General recommendations for ages 0 to 6 years (age listed in months):

Age in months ▶ Vaccine ▼	0	1	2	4	6
Hepatitis B	☑	☑			☑
Rotavirus			☑	☑	☑
DTaP			☑	☑	☑
Hib			☑	☑	☑
Pneumococcal			☑	☑	☑

Age in months ▶ / Vaccine ▼	0	1	2	4	6
IPV			☑	☑	
Influenza					☑
MMR					
Varicella					
Hepatitis A					
Meningococcal					

Age in months ▶ / Vaccine ▼	12	15	18	19–23	24–36	48–72
Hepatitis B						
Rotavirus						
DTaP			☑			☑
Hib		☑				
Pneumococcal	☑					
IPV		☑				☑
Influenza				☑		
MMR	☑	☑				☑

continued

Age in months ▶ Vaccine ▼	12	15	18	19–23	24–36	48–72
Varicella	☑	☑				☑
Hepatitis A	2 doses					
Meningococcal					High-risk pts.	

Lab Procedures

Blood Tests

Draw order

Collection tubes must be filled in a specific order to preserve the integrity of the blood sample.

Preparing a blood smear

Critical Procedure Steps

1. Wash your hands and put on exam gloves.

2. If you will be using blood from a capillary puncture, express a drop of blood from the patient's finger. If you will be using a venous sample, check the specimen for proper labeling, carefully uncap the specimen tube, and use wooden applicator sticks to remove any coagulated blood from the inside rim of the tube. You may use a special safety transfer device if available.

3. Touch the tip of the capillary tube to the blood specimen either from the patient's finger or the specimen tube. The tube will take up the correct amount through capillary action.

4. Pull the capillary tube away from the sample, holding it carefully to prevent spillage. Wipe the outside of the capillary tube with a sterile gauze square.

5. With the slide on the work surface, hold the capillary tube in one hand and the frosted end of the slide against the work surface with the other.

6. Apply a drop of blood to the slide, about ¾ inch from the frosted end. Place the capillary tube in the sharps container.

7. Pick up the spreader slide with your dominant hand. Hold the slide at approximately a 30- to 35-degree angle. Place the edge of the spreader slide on the smear slide close to the unfrosted end. Pull the spreader slide toward the frosted end until the spreader slide touches the blood drop. Capillary action will spread the droplet along the edge of the spreader slide.

8. As soon as the drop spreads out to cover most of the spreader slide edge, push the spreader slide back toward the unfrosted end of the smear slide, pulling the sample across the slide behind it. Maintain the 30- to 35-degree angle.

continued

9. Continue pushing the spreader until you come off the end, still maintaining the angle. The resulting smear should be approximately 1½ inches long, preferably with a margin of empty slide on all sides. The smear should be thicker on the frosted end of the slide.

10. Properly label the slide, allow it to dry, and follow the manufacturer's directions for staining it for the required tests.

11. Properly dispose of used supplies, and disinfect the work area.

12. Remove the gloves and wash your hands.

Quality control

Critical Procedure Steps

1. Review the test form for the test ordered and verify the procedure.

2. Prepare the equipment, paperwork, and work area.

3. Identify the patient and explain the procedure.

4. Confirm that the patient has followed any pretest preparation requirements.

5. Collect the specimen properly.

6. Use the correct specimen collection containers and the right additives, if required.

7. Immediately label the specimens.

8. Follow correct procedure for disposing of biohazardous waste.
9. Keep the patient in the office for follow-up observation if required.
10. Properly prepare the specimen for transport to an outside lab if indicated.

Tube additives and colors

When drawing multiple tubes of blood, you should collect them in the order listed below. This reduces the chance of cross contaminating the tube additives.

Stopper Color	Additive
Yellow	Sodium polyanetholsulfonate
Light blue	Sodium citrate
Red	None
Gold or red/black	Silicone serum separator
Green	Heparin
Lavender	Ethylenediaminetetraacetic acid (EDTA) (anticoagulant)
Gray	Potassium oxalate or sodium fluoride (anticoagulant)

Causes of Lab Errors
- Improperly calibrated equipment
- Reagents out of date
- Contaminated reagents

- Controls not done or improperly done
- Improperly performed testing procedure
- Incorrect timing
- Improperly collected sample
- Incorrect interpretation of results

Common Lab Tests (Waived Tests)

Urine tests	Urinalysis by dipstick (reagent strip) or tablet reagent (nonautomated) for bilirubin, glucose, hemoglobin, ketone, leukocytes, nitrite, pH, protein, specific gravity, and urobilinogen
	Ovulation (visual color comparison tests)
	Pregnancy (visual color comparison tests)
	Home-screening tests for drugs (opioids, cocaine, methamphetamines, cannabinoids)
	Nicotine detection tests
	Urine chemistry analyzer for microalbumin and creatinine (semi-quantitative)
	Tumor-associated antigen for bladder cancer (using devices approved by the FDA for home use)
	Catalase

Blood tests	Erythrocyte sedimentation rate (ESR), nonautomated
	Hemoglobin by copper sulfate, nonautomated
	Spun microhematocrit
	Blood glucose (using devices approved by the FDA for home use)
	Hemoglobin by single analyte instruments, automated
	Prothrombin time
	Ketones in whole blood, OTC test only
	Total cholesterol, HDL, LDL, and triglycerides
	Hemoglobin A1c
	Lactate in whole blood
	Lead in whole blood
	Thyroid-stimulating hormone, rapid test
	Mononucleosis rapid test
	Helicobacter pylori rapid antibody test

Source: Reprinted courtesy of the U.S. Department of Health and Human Services.

Collection Techniques

Capillary puncture

Critical Procedure Steps

1. Review the laboratory request and gather the supplies.
2. Identify the patient.
3. Explain the procedure; confirm that the patient has followed the pretest procedures.
4. Position the patient in the venipuncture chair or lying down.
5. Wash your hands and put on gloves.
6. Examine the patient's hands to determine which finger to use. Generally, the middle two fingers.
7. Gently massage the finger.
8. Clean the area with antiseptic.
9. Hold the patient's finger between your thumb and forefinger.
10. Puncture the finger with a safety lancet.
11. Allow a drop of blood to form at the end of the patient's finger.
12. Wipe away the first drop of blood.
13. Fill the collection device.
14. Dispose of the lancet.
15. Wipe the patient's finger with a sterile gauze square.

16. Have the patient apply pressure to the puncture site.

17. Label the specimen and complete the laboratory request form or perform the test.

18. Check the puncture site for bleeding.

19. Properly dispose of used supplies and disposable instruments.

20. Remove the gloves and wash your hands.

21. Instruct the patient about care of the puncture site.

22. Document the procedure and record the results if appropriate.

Venipuncture

Critical Procedure Steps

1. Review the laboratory request form and gather the supplies.

2. Identify the patient.

3. Explain the procedure; confirm that the patient has followed the pretest procedures.

4. Position the patient in the venipuncture chair or lying down.

5. Wash your hands and put on gloves.

6. Insert the threaded end of the needle into the safety needle holder and push the first collection tube part way into the holder.

continued

7. Position the patient's arm slightly downward.

8. Apply the tourniquet to the patient's upper arm midway between the elbow and shoulder.

9. Palpate the proposed site with your index finger to locate the vein.

10. Clean the area with an antiseptic wipe using a circular motion.

11. Remove the plastic cap from the outer point of the needle, ask the patient to make a fist, and pull the skin taut below the insertion site.

12. Insert the needle at a 15-degree angle, bevel side up.

13. Seat the collection tube in place on the needle, puncturing the rubber stopper. Fill the tube.

14. Once blood flow is steady, have the patient release his fist and untie the tourniquet.

15. Withdraw the needle with a smooth, steady motion and place a sterile gauze square over the insertion site.

16. Immediately activate the safety device.

17. Ask the patient to hold pressure at the site.

18. Slowly invert the collection tubes if they contain additives.

19. Label the specimens and complete the paperwork.

20. Observe the patient's condition and check the site for bleeding.

21. Place a sterile adhesive bandage over the puncture site.
22. Properly dispose of used supplies and disposable instruments.
23. Remove the gloves and wash your hands.
24. Instruct the patient about care of the puncture site.
25. Document the procedure in the patient's chart.

Venipuncture complications

Complication	Tips for Avoiding Complications
Hematoma	• Hold the needle as still as possible • Use a butterfly system for small veins • Hold pressure at the puncture site as soon as you remove the needle
Infection	• Use only approved single-use equipment • Clean the puncture site thoroughly
Latex allergy	• Before the procedure, ask the patient if they have any allergies • Use non-latex gloves, tourniquets, and bandages
Nerve Injury	Review the anatomy of the antecubital fossa prior to performing the procedure

Special considerations

- Children—address the child directly; speaking in a calm, soothing voice, briefly explain the procedure
- Difficult venipuncture—if your first attempt fails, try another site. Ask for assistance after two attempts.
- Elderly patients—speak in low, clear tones. Take your time with the procedure.
- Fainting—position the patient in a venipuncture chair so that, if they do faint, no injury will occur
- Patients at risk for uncontrolled bleeding

Common Abbreviations

cm = centimeter

cm^3 = cubic centimeter

dL = deciliter

fl oz = fluid ounce

g = gram

L = liter

lb = pound

m = meter

mcg = microgram

mg = milligram

mL = milliliter

mm = millimeter

mm Hg = millimeters of mercury

oz = ounce

pt = pint

QNS = quantity not sufficient

QS = quantity sufficient

qt = quart

U = unit

wt = weight

Labeled Microscope and Tips

Care and cleaning

- Clean the microscope after each use.
- Inspect the body tube, arm, and stage for dust and other contaminants.
- Clean the oculars and lenses with lens paper, not tissue.
- Use lens cleaning products according to manufacturer's guidelines.
- Store the microscope with the cover on and the cord wrapped loosely around the base.
- Carry the microscope with one hand on the arm and one supporting the base.

Identification

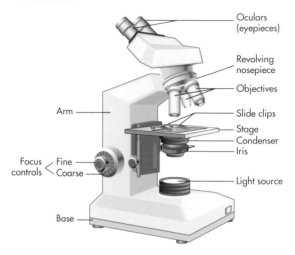

Oculars (eyepieces)

Revolving nosepiece

Objectives

Arm

Slide clips

Stage

Condenser

Iris

Focus controls { Fine Coarse

Light source

Base

Using a microscope

Critical Procedure Steps

1. Wash your hands and put on gloves.
2. Examine the microscope to make sure it is clean and all parts are intact.
3. Plug the microscope in and make sure the light is working.
4. Turn the light off and clean the lenses with lens paper.

5. Place the specimen slide on the stage and secure it in place.

6. Position distance between the oculars to a position of comfort.

7. Adjust the 10X objective so it points directly at the specimen leaving enough space so that the slide does not touch the objective.

8. Turn on the light and adjust the iris so that light fills the field without washing it out.

9. Observe the slide from one side and adjust the body tube to move the objective closer to the specimen.

10. Use the coarse focus to slowly bring the image into focus.

11. Use the fine focus until the image is clearly visible.

12. Switch to the 40X objective and refocus using the fine focus.

13. Rotate the objective assembly so that no objective points at the specimen.

14. Add a drop of immersion oil to the slide.

15. Rotate the 100X objective into the oil.

16. Examine the image and adjust the light and focus using the fine focus only as needed.

17. After examining the specimen, lower the stage and raise the objectives.

18. Remove the slide and dispose of it or store it.

continued

19. Turn off the light and unplug the microscope according to office policy.

20. Carefully clean the stage, ocular lenses, and objectives, removing all traces of immersion oil.

21. Point the 10X objective toward the stage and lower it so it is close but not touching the stage.

22. Cover the microscope and clean the area.

23. Remove your gloves and wash your hands.

Lab Slip Completion

YOU SHOULD KNOW

When completing a laboratory requisition slip, you should include the following information:

- Patient's full name, sex, date of birth, and address
- Patient's insurance information
- Physician's name, address, and phone number
- Source of the specimen
- Date and time of the specimen collection
- Test(s) requested
- Preliminary diagnosis
- Any current treatment that might affect the results

Microbiology Review

Classification of microorganisms

- Bacteria—single-celled, prokaryotic organisms
- Fungi—eukaryotic organisms with a rigid cell wall
- Multicellular parasites—organisms that live on or in another organism and use that other organism for their own nourishment, or for some other advantage, to the detriment of the host organism.
- Protozoans—single-celled, eukaryotic organisms usually larger than bacteria
- Viruses—consist of nucleic acid and a protein coat

Diagnosing and treating infections

The basic steps include:

- Examining the patient
- Obtaining specimens
- Examining the specimens directly
- Culturing the specimen
- Determining the culture's antibiotic sensitivity
- Treating the patient as ordered by the physician

Obtaining a throat culture

Critical Procedure Steps

1. Identify the patient and explain the procedure.
2. Assemble the necessary supplies and label the culture plate if used.
3. Wash your hands and put on gloves, goggles, and a mask or face shield.

continued

4. Have the patient assume a sitting position.

5. Open the collection system or swab package and remove the swab with your dominant hand.

6. Ask the patient to tilt her head back and open her mouth as wide as possible.

7. With your other hand, depress the patient's tongue with a tongue depressor.

8. Ask the patient to say "Ah."

9. Insert the swab and quickly swab the area of the tonsils.

10. Remove the swab and then the tongue depressor from the patient's mouth.

11. Discard the tongue depressor in the biohazard container.

12. Immediately insert the swab into the plastic sleeve or inoculate the culture plate as required by the test.

13. Crush the vial of transport media or discard after inoculating the culture plate.

14. Label the specimen and arrange for transport to the laboratory or place the plate in the incubator.

Specimen collection guidelines

YOU SHOULD KNOW

- Obtain the specimen with great care to avoid causing the patient harm, discomfort, or undue embarrassment.

- Collect the material from a site where the organism is most likely to be found and where contamination is least likely to occur

- Obtain the specimen at a time that allows optimal chance of recovery of the microorganism.

- Use appropriate collection devices, specimen containers, transport systems, and culture media to ensure optimal recovery of microorganisms.

- Obtain a sufficient quantity of the specimen for performing the requested procedures.

- Obtain the specimen before antimicrobial therapy begins.

Transporting to an outside laboratory

Critical Procedure Steps

1. Wash your hands and put on gloves.
2. Obtain the microbiologic culture specimen.
3. Use the collection system specified by the outside laboratory.
4. Label the collection device at the time of collection.
5. Collect the specimen according to the guidelines provided by the laboratory and office policy.

continued

6. Remove the gloves and wash your hands.

7. Complete the requisition form.

8. Place the specimen container in a secondary zipper-type plastic bag.

9. Attach the test requisition form to the outside of the secondary container or bag.

10. Store the specimen according to the laboratory guidelines for the type of specimen.

11. Call the laboratory for pickup.

12. At the time of pickup ensure that all specimens that are logged in are picked up.

13. If you are unsure of collection or transport details, call the laboratory.

MSDS

The following information about chemicals can be found on a standard MSDS:

- Substance name
- Chemical name
- Common name
- Chemical characteristics
- Physical hazards
- Health hazards
- Guidelines for safe handling
- Emergency and first-aid procedures

Normal Values

Blood tests

Blood Test	Normal Range
Blood Counts	
Red blood cells	
Men	4.3–5.7×10^6 cells/mcL
Women	3.8–5.1×10^6 cells/mcL
White blood cells	4.5–11.0×10^3 cells/mcL
Platelets	150–400×10^3 cells/mcL
Differential	
Neutrophils	60%–70%
Eosinophils	1%–4%
Basophils	0%–0.5%
Lymphocytes	20%–30%
Monocytes	2%–6%
Hemoglobin	
Men	13.2–17.3 g/dL
Women	11.7–16.0 g/dL
Erythrocyte sedimentation rate	
Wintrobe	
Men	0–5 mm/hour
Women	0–15 mm/hour
Westergren	
Men	0–15 mm/hour
Women	0–20 mm/hour

continued

Blood Test	Normal Range
Coagulation tests	
Prothrombin	11–15 seconds
Bleeding time	2–7 minutes
Electrolytes	
Bicarbonate	27–29 mEq/L
Calcium	8.6–10.0 mEq/L
Chloride	98–108 mEq/L
Potassium	3.5–5.1 mEq/L
Sodium	136–145 mEq/L
Chemical and serologic	
Alpha-fetoprotein	
Fetal, first trimester	20–400 mg/dL
Adult	<15 ng/mL
Alanine aminotransferase	
Men	10–40 U/L
Women	7–35 U/L
Aspartate aminotransferase	
Men	11–26 U/L
Women	10–20 U/L
Bilirubin	0.3–1.2 mg/dL
Blood urea nitrogen (BUN)	6–20 mg/dL

Blood Test	Normal Range
Carcinoembryonic antigen	<5.0 ng/mL
Cholesterol, total	
Men	158–277 mg/dL
Women	162–285 mg/dL
HDL	
Men	28–63 mg/dL
Women	37–92 mg/dL
LDL	
Men	89–197 mg/dL
Women	88–201 mg/dL
Creatine kinase	
Men	38–174 U/L
Women	26–140 U/L
Creatinine	
Men	0.9–1.3 mg/dL
Women	0.6–1.2 mg/dL
Cytomegalovirus	None
Epstein-Barr virus	None
Glucose (FBS)	74–120 mg/dL
Group A strep	None
HIV	None
Insulin	<17 mcU/mL

continued

Blood Test	Normal Range
Iron, total	
Men	65–175 mcg/dL
Women	50–170 mcg/dL
Lactate dehydrogenase	140–280 U/L
pH	7.32–7.43
Proteins	
Total	6.2–8.0 g/dL
Albumin	3.4–4.8 g/dL
Fibrinogen	200–400 mg/dL
Uric acid	
Men	4.4–7.6 mg/dL
Women	2.3–6.6 mg/dL

Various laboratories may have different normal reference ranges than those represented in this table. Consult your laboratory procedures manual for additional information regarding normal ranges.

Urinalysis

Physical Characteristics	
Test	**Normal values**
Color	Pale yellow–yellow
Clarity	Clear–slightly turbid

Reagent Strip Test	
Test	**Normal values**
Bilirubin	Negative
Blood	Negative
Glucose	Negative
Ketone bodies (Acetone)	Negative
Leukocytes	Negative
Nitrites	Negative
pH	4.5–8.0
Protein	Negative–trace
Specific gravity	1.002–1.028
Urobilinogen	0.3–1.0 E. U.

Microscopic Examination	
Test	**Normal value**
Bacteria	Negative
Casts	
Epithelial cell	Negative
Granular	Negative
Hyaline	Few
Red blood cell	Negative
Waxy	Negative
White blood cell	Negative

continued

Microscopic Examination

Test	Normal value
Crystals	
Amorphous phosphates	Normal
Calcium carbonate	Normal
Calcium oxalate	Normal
Cholesterol	Negative
Cystine	Negative
Leucine	Negative
Sulfonamide	Negative
Triple phosphate	Normal
Tyrosine	Negative
Uric acid	Normal
Epithelial cells	
Renal	Negative
Squamous, adult females	Moderate
Squamous, adult males	Few
Transitional	Rare
Mucus	Rare – few
Protozoa	Negative
Red blood cells	0–3/high-power field
White blood cells	0–8/high-power field
Yeast	Few

24 hour	
Test	**Normal Value**
5HIAA	2–8 mg
Albumin (quantitative)	10–140 mg/L
Ammonia	140–1500 mg
Calcium, (quantitative)	100–300 mg
Atecholamines, total	<100 mcg
Chloride	110–120 mEq
Cortisol	10 to 100 mcg
Creatine, nonpregnant women/men	<100 mcg
Creatine, pregnant women	≤12% of creatinine
Creatinine, men	1.0–1.9 g
Creatinine, women	0.8–1.7 g
Cystine and cysteine	<38.1 mg
Glucose, quantitative	50–500 mg
Phosphorus	0.4–1.3 g
Potassium	25–120 mEq/L
Protein (Bence Jones)	Negative
Sodium	80–180 mEq

continued

24 hour	
Test	**Normal Value**
Urea nitrogen	6–17 g
Uric acid	0.25–0.75 g
Urobilinogen, quantitative	1.0–4.0 mg
Volume, adult females	600–1600 mL
Volume, adult males	800–1800 mL
Volume, children	3–4 times adult rate/kg

Individual laboratories may have slightly different reference values. Consult the reference values provided by the lab performing the test.

Safety

Accident reporting guidelines for reporting blood and body fluid exposure

1. Immediate cleaning of the area, including disinfection of contaminated surfaces and sterilization of contaminated instruments and equipment
2. Notification of a designated emergency contact, as identified in your office's safety manual
3. Documentation of the incident on a form, including the names of all parties involved, the names of witnesses, a description of the incident, and a record of medical treatments given to those involved
4. Medical evaluation and follow-up exam of the employees involved

5. Written evaluation of the medical condition of the involved individuals as well as testing for infection, provided that such testing does not violate confidentiality regulations

Biologic safety

- Follow Standard Precautions.
- If you have cuts, lesions, or sores, do not expose yourself to potentially contaminated material.
- Wash your hands before and after every procedure.
- Wear gloves at all times. Wear other protective gear as appropriate.
- Always use an approved pipette device to transfer fluids. Never pipette by mouth.
- Work in a biologic safety cabinet when splashes or sprays are possible.
- When transferring a blood sample from one container to another, take care when opening the tube. Open the tube away from your face.
- Establish clean and dirty areas in the laboratory.
- Disinfect work area with 10% bleach at least once a day.
- Dispose of waste materials immediately.
- Dispose of sharps in approved containers.
- Decontaminate equipment prior to servicing
- If you use a bleach solution for disinfection, change it daily.

Chemical safety

- Wear protective gear.
- Carry chemical containers with both hands.

- Work in a properly ventilated area.
- If you must smell a chemical, hold it away from your nose and fan air across the container toward your nose.
- Work inside a fume hood if the chemical vapor is hazardous.
- Wear a personal ventilation device when indicated by the MSDS.
- Never combine chemicals in ways not specifically required in test procedures.
- Always use an approved pipette device to transfer fluids. Never pipette by mouth.
- If you are combining acid with other substances, always add acid to the other substance.
- Clean up spills according to strict hazardous waste control procedures.
- Never touch an unknown chemical substance with your bare hands.

Electric safety

- Avoid using extension cords.
- Repair or replace equipment that has a broken or frayed cord.
- Dry your hands before working with electrical devices.
- Do not position electrical devices near sinks, faucets, or other sources of water.

Fire safety

- Extinguish an open flame immediately after use.
- Keep hair, clothing, and jewelry away from an open flame.

- When using a chemical near an open flame, check the MSDS to identify the level of risk of fire for that chemical.
- Never lean over an open flame.
- Never leave an open flame unattended.
- Turn off gas valves immediately after use.

Needlestick safety

- Health-care employers must evaluate new safety-engineered control devices on an annual basis and implement the use of devices that reasonably reduce the risk of needlestick injuries.
- Health-care facilities must maintain a detailed log of sharps injuries that are incurred from contaminated sharps.
- Health-care employers must solicit input from employees involved in direct patient care to identify, evaluate, and implement engineering and work practice controls.

Physical safety

- Walk, do not run, in the laboratory.
- Close all cabinet and closet doors and all desk and worktable drawers.
- Never use damaged equipment or supplies.
- Do not overextend your reach when attempting to grasp supplies.
- Do not climb onto chairs, desks, or tables to reach anything.
- Lift with your legs when lifting heavy objects.
- Adjust your seat to the correct position to avoid back strain.

- Do not eat or drink in the laboratory.
- Do not put anything in your mouth while working in the laboratory.
- Do not apply makeup or lip balm or insert contact lenses in the laboratory.
- Know the location of the first-aid kit.
- Know the location and proper use of the eyewash and shower stations.

Slide Staining Techniques

Gram's stain

Critical Procedure Steps

1. Assemble all necessary supplies.
2. Wash your hands and put on gloves.
3. Place the heat-fixed smear on a level staining rack and tray.
4. Completely cover the specimen area with crystal violet stain.
5. Allow the stain to sit for 1 minute, wash with water.
6. Using forceps, tilt the slide to one side to drain the excess water.
7. Place the slide flat on the rack again and cover with iodine solution.
8. Allow the iodine to sit for 1 minute, wash with water.
9. Tilt the slide to drain the excess water.

10. With the slide tilted, apply the alcohol drop by drop until no more purple washes off (10–30 seconds).

11. Wash the slide with water then tilt it to remove excess water.

12. Return the slide to the rack and cover with safranin stain.

13. Allow the safranin to sit for 1 minute, and then wash with water.

14. Carefully wipe the back of the slide to remove excess stain.

15. Place the slide in the vertical position and allow to air dry or blot with blotting paper.

16. Sanitize and disinfect the work area.

17. Remove the gloves and wash your hands.

Troubleshooting Lab Procedures

General steps

- Have a written procedure for troubleshooting tests and equipment.
- Recognize the problem (controls give clues to possible problems).
- Think about possible causes.
- Start with the simplest cause first.
- Document your findings.
- Call your service company after you have checked everything you know to check.

Laboratory equipment

- Check the power source at the machine, the wall outlet, the breaker box, or the battery.
- Check the equipment manual for troubleshooting information.
- Reboot the equipment by turning it off, waiting a few minutes, and then turning it back on.
- Check the service log for the date of the last maintenance.
- If you are able to repair the problem, run controls to verify the problem is fixed before testing patient samples.

Laboratory test kits

- Read the package insert to verify you have performed the test correctly.
- Check to make sure you have used the correct reagents or test strips.
- Check the dates on the reagents or test strips to make sure they are not outdated.
- Make sure you are using the proper sample for the test.
- Repeat the test using control samples.
- If the controls are correct, repeat the test with the patient sample.

Urine

Characteristics

- **Color and turbidity**—assess for color and cloudiness
- **Odor**—should be aromatic but not unpleasant

- **Specific gravity**—a measure of the concentration or amount of substances dissolved in urine.
- **Volume**—usually measured on a timed specimen

Collecting a clean catch midstream urine specimen

Critical Procedure Steps

1. Confirm the patient's identity and be sure all forms are correctly completed.

2. Label the sterile urine specimen container with the patient's name, ID number, date of birth, the physician's name, the date and time of collection, and the initials of the person collecting the specimen.

When the patient will be completing the procedure independently:

3. Explain the procedure in detail. Provide the patient with written instructions, antiseptic towelettes, and the labeled sterile specimen container.

4. Confirm that the patient understands the instructions, especially not to touch the inside of the specimen container and to refrigerate the specimen until bringing it to the physician's office.

When you are assisting a patient:

3. Explain the procedure and how you will be assisting in the collection.

continued

4. Wash your hands and put on exam gloves.

When you are assisting in the collection for female patients:

5. Remove the lid from the specimen container, and place the lid upside down on a flat surface.

6. Use three antiseptic towelettes to clean the perineal area by spreading the labia and wiping from front to back. Wipe with the first towelette on one side and discard it. Wipe with the second towelette on the other side and discard it. Wipe with the third towelette down the middle and discard it. To remove soap residue that could cause a higher pH and affect chemical test results, rinse the area once from front to back with water.

7. Keeping the patient's labia spread to avoid contamination, tell her to urinate into the toilet. After she has expressed a small amount of urine, instruct her to stop the flow.

8. Position the specimen container close to but not touching the patient.

9. Tell the patient to start urinating again. Collect the necessary amount of urine in the container. (If the patient cannot stop her urine flow, move the container into the urine flow and collect the specimen anyway.)

10. Allow the patient to finish urinating. Place the lid back on the collection container.

11. Remove the gloves and wash your hands.

12. Complete the test request slip, and record the collection in the patient's chart.

When you are assisting in the collection for male patients:

5. Remove the lid from the specimen container, and place the lid upside down on a flat surface.

6. If the patient is circumcised, use an antiseptic towelette to clean the head of the penis. Wipe with a second towelette directly across the urethral opening. If the patient is uncircumcised, retract the foreskin before cleaning the penis. To remove soap residue that could cause a higher pH and affect chemical test results, rinse the area once from front to back with water.

7. Keeping an uncircumcised patient's foreskin retracted, tell the patient to urinate into the toilet. After he has expressed a small amount of urine, instruct him to stop the flow.

8. Position the specimen container close to but not touching the patient.

9. Tell the patient to start urinating again. Collect the necessary amount of urine in the container. (If the patient cannot stop his urine flow, move the container into the urine flow and collect the specimen anyway.)

10. Allow the patient to finish urinating. Place the lid back on the collection container.

continued

11. Remove the gloves and wash your hands.

12. Complete the laboratory request form, and record the collection in the patient's chart

Collecting a urine specimen from a pediatric patient

Critical Procedure Steps

1. Confirm the patient's identity and be sure all forms are correctly completed.

2. Label the urine specimen container with the patient's name, ID number, and date of birth, the physician's name, the date and time of collection, and your initials.

3. Explain the procedure to the child (if age-appropriate) and to the parents or guardians.

4. Wash your hands and put on exam gloves.

5. Have the parents pull the child's pants down and take off the diaper.

6. Position the child with the genitalia exposed.

7. Clean the genitalia. For a male patient, wipe the tip of the penis with a soapy cotton ball, and then rinse it with a cotton ball saturated with sterile water. Allow to air-dry. For a female patient, use soapy cotton balls to clean the labia majora from front to back, using one cotton ball for each wipe. Again, use cotton balls saturated in sterile

water to rinse the area, and allow it to air-dry.

8. Remove the paper backing from the plastic urine collection bag, and apply the sticky, adhesive surface over the penis and scrotum (in a male patient) or vulva (in a female patient). Seal tightly to avoid leaks. Do not include the child's rectum within the collection bag or cover it with the adhesive surface.

9. Diaper the child.

10. Remove the gloves and wash your hands.

11. Check the collection bag every half-hour for urine. You must open the diaper to check; do not just feel the diaper.

12. If the child has voided, wash your hands and put on exam gloves.

13. Remove the diaper, take off the urine collection bag very carefully so that you do not irritate the child's skin, wash off the adhesive residue, rinse, and pat dry.

14. Diaper the child.

15. Place the specimen in the specimen container and cover it.

16. Remove the gloves and wash your hands.

17. Complete the laboratory request form, and record the collection in the patient's chart.

Color and turbidity: Possible causes

Color and Turbidity	Possible Cause
Colorless or pale	Diabetes, anxiety, chronic renal disease, diuretic therapy, excessive fluid intake
Cloudy	Infection, inflammation, glomerular nephritis, vegetarian diet
Milky white	Fats, pus, amorphous phosphates, spermatozoa
Dark yellow, dark amber	Acute febrile disease, vomiting or diarrhea, low fluid intake, excessive sweating
Yellow-brown	Excessive RBC destruction, bile duct obstruction, diminished liver-cell function, bilirubin
Orange-yellow, orange-red, orange-brown	Excessive RBC destruction, diminished liver-cell function, bile, hepatitis, urobilinuria, obstructive jaundice, hematuria
Salmon pink	Amorphous urates
Cloudy red	RBCs, excessive destruction of skeletal or cardiac muscle
Bright yellow or red	RBCs, excessive destruction of skeletal or cardiac muscle, porphyria, beets, some drugs, dyes
Dark red, red-brown	Porphyria, RBCs, blood from previous hemorrhage

Color and Turbidity	Possible Cause
Green, blue-green	Biliverdin, *Pseudomonas* organisms, oxidation of bilirubin
Green-brown	Bile duct obstruction
Brownish black	Methemoglobin, melanin, some drugs
Dark brown or black	Acute glomerulonephritis, some drugs

Dipstick testing method

Critical Procedure Steps

1. Wash your hands and put on gloves.
2. Check the specimen for proper labeling and visible contaminants.
3. Check the expiration date on the strips.
4. Check the strip for damage.
5. Complete the test within one hour of collecting the sample or refrigerate the sample until the test can be performed.
6. Swirl the sample.
7. Dip the strip in the urine, completely covering the strip.
8. Tap the strip sideways on a paper towel but do not blot it.

continued

9. Read the strip against the chart at the designated time.

10. Record the values on the laboratory report form.

11. Discard the used disposable supplies.

12. Clean and disinfect the work area.

13. Remove your gloves and wash your hands.

14. Record the results in the patient's chart.

Establishing a chain of custody

Critical Procedure Steps

1. Positively identify the patient. (Complete the top part of Chain of Custody Form with the name and address of the drug-testing laboratory, the name and address of requesting company, and the Social Security number of the patient. Make a note on the form if the patient refuses to give her Social Security number.) Ensure that the number on the printed label matches the number at the top of the form.

2. Ensure that the patient removes any outer clothing and empties her pockets, displaying all items.

3. Instruct the patient to wash and dry her hands.

4. Instruct the patient that no water is to be running while the specimen is being collected.

Tape the faucet handles in the *off* position and add bluing agent to the toilet.

5. Instruct the patient to provide the specimen as soon as it is collected so that you may record the temperature of the specimen.

6. Remain by the door of the restroom.

7. Measure and record the temperature of the urine specimen within 4 minutes of collection. Make a note if its temperature is out of acceptable range.

8. Examine the specimen for signs of adulteration (unusual color or odor).

9. *In the presence of the patient,* check the "single specimen" or "split specimen" box. The patient should witness you transferring the specimen into the transport specimen bottle(s), capping the bottle(s), and affixing the label on the bottle(s).

10. The patient should initial the specimen bottle label(s) *after* it is placed on the bottle(s).

11. Complete any additional information requested on the form, including the authorization for drug screening. This information will include:
    • Patient's daytime telephone number
    • Patient's evening telephone number
    • Test requested
    • Patient's name
    • Patient's signature
    • Date

continued

12. Sign the CCF; print your full name, note the date and time of the collection, and the name of the courier service.
13. Give the patient a copy of the CCF.
14. Place the specimen in a leakproof bag with the appropriate copy of the form.
15. Release the specimen to the courier service.
16. Distribute additional copies as required.

Microscopic components

The microscopic components of urine include:

- Bacteria
- Casts
- Cells
- Crystals
- Parasites
- Yeasts

Spinning

1. Wash your hands and put on gloves.
2. Check the specimen for proper labeling and visible contaminants.
3. Complete the test within one hour of collecting the sample or refrigerate the sample until the test can be performed.
4. Swirl the sample.
5. Pour 10 mL of the urine in one test tube.
6. Place the tube in the centrifuge and balance with another tube filled with 10 mL of water.

7. Secure the centrifuge lid and set the timer.

8. Set the speed according to office protocol and start the centrifuge.

9. After the centrifuge stops lift the tube and carefully pour off the liquid.

10. Tap to resuspend the sediment in the drops of urine left in the bottom of the tube.

11. Use a pipette to remove a few drops of the urine sediment.

12. Place the drops on a clean slide and cover with a coverslip.

13. Place the slide on the microscope stage and focus the image.

14. Alert the physician that the slide has been prepared and is ready for her examination.

Medication Administration

7 Rights of Drug Administration

YOU SHOULD KNOW

1. **Right patient**—always check the name and date of birth of the patient.

2. **Right drug**—compare the name of the prescribed drug in the patient's chart with the drug container label. Check three times!

3. **Right dose**—compare the dose ordered with the dose you prepare.

continued

4. **Right time**—give the drug at the prescribed time.

5. **Right route**—make sure the administration route you have prepared matches the prescribed route.

6. **Right technique**—use the proper administration technique.

7. **Right documentation**—document immediately after administering the drug.

Types of Drug Administration

Administering buccal or sublingual drugs

Critical Procedure Steps

1. Identify the patient and wash your hands.

2. Select the ordered drug.

3. Check the 7 Rights.

4. If you are unfamiliar with the drug, check the PDR, read the package insert, or speak with the physician.

5. Ask the patient about drug or food allergies.

6. Perform calculations needed to provide the prescribed dose.

7. Open the container and tap the correct number into the cap.

8. Tap the tablets or capsules into a paper cup.

9. Recap the container immediately.

10. Tell the patient not to chew or swallow.

11. *Buccal*—place the medication between the cheek and the gum until it dissolves. *Sublingual*—place the medication under the tongue until it dissolves.

12. Instruct the patient not to eat, drink, or smoke until the tablet is completely dissolved.

13. Remain with the patient until the tablet dissolves.

14. Wash your hands.

15. Give the patient written and oral information about the drug and answer any questions.

16. Document the date, time, drug name, dosage, expiration date, lot number, manufacturer, route, site, significant patient reactions, and patient education in the chart.

Administering eardrops

Critical Procedure Steps

1. Identify the patient and explain the procedure.

2. Review the medication order.

3. Compare the drug with the medication order three times.

4. Ask the patient about drug allergies.

5. Wash your hands and put on gloves.

6. Assemble the supplies.

continued

7. Warm the medication to room temperature.

8. Have the patient lie on her side with the affected ear up.

9. Straighten the ear canal by pulling upward and outward for adults or down and back for infants and children.

10. Hold the dropper ½ inch from the ear canal.

11. Gently squeeze the dropper or bottle to administer the ordered number of drops.

12. Have the patient remain in this position for 10 minutes.

13. If ordered, loosely place a small cotton ball in the patient's ear.

14. Observe for adverse reactions.

15. Repeat the procedure for the other ear if indicated.

16. Instruct the patient on how to administer the drops at home.

17. Provide written instructions.

18. Remove the cotton after 15 minutes.

19. Properly dispose of disposable supplies.

20. Remove the gloves and wash your hands.

21. Document the date, time, drug name, number of drops, drug concentration, expiration date, lot number, manufacturer, route, site, significant patient reactions, and patient education in the chart.

Administering eye medications

Critical Procedure Steps

1. Identify the patient and explain the procedure.
2. Review the medication order.
3. Compare the drug with the medication order three times.
4. Ask the patient about drug allergies.
5. Wash your hands and put on gloves.
6. Assemble the supplies.
7. Ask the patient to lie down or sit with her head tilted back.
8. Give the patient a tissue to blot excess medication as needed.
9. Remove an eye patch, if present.
10. Ask the patient to look at the ceiling and keep both eyes open during the procedure.
11. With a tissue, gently pull the lower eyelid down creating a pocket.

Eyedrops

12. Rest your dominant hand on the patient's forehead holding the filled eyedropper or bottle ½ inch from the conjunctiva.
13. Drop the prescribed number of drops in the pocket.

continued

Creams or Ointments

12. Rest your dominant hand on the patient's forehead holding the tube or applicator above the conjunctiva.

13. Without touching the eyelid or conjunctiva with the applicator, apply a thin ribbon of cream or ointment along the inside edge of the lower eyelid, working from the inner to the outer side.

All Medications

14. Release the lower lid and instruct the patient to gently close her eyes.

15. Repeat the procedure for the other eye if indicated.

16. Remove any excess medication by wiping each eyelid with a tissue from the inner to the outer side.

17. Apply a clean eye patch if necessary.

18. Ask if the patient felt any discomfort and observe for adverse reactions.

19. Instruct the patient on self-administration of medication and patch application as necessary.

20. Ask the patient to repeat the instructions.

21. Provide written instructions.

22. Properly dispose of disposable supplies.

23. Remove the gloves and wash your hands.

24. Document the date, time, drug name, number of drops, drug concentration, expiration

date, lot number, manufacturer, route, site, significant patient reactions, and patient education in the chart.

Administering oral drugs

Critical Procedure Steps

1. Identify the patient and wash your hands.
2. Select the ordered drug.
3. Check the 7 Rights.
4. If you are unfamiliar with the drug, check the PDR, read the package insert, or speak with the physician.
5. Ask the patient about drug or food allergies.
6. Perform calculations needed to provide the prescribed dose.

Tablets or Capsules

7. Open the container and tap the correct number into the cap.
8. Tap the tablets or capsules into a paper cup.
9. Recap the container immediately.
10. Give the patient the cup and a glass of water or juice.

Liquid

7. Shake a liquid suspension.

continued

8. Locate the correct mark on the medicine cup and pour in the correct amount of medication. Place your palm over the label so that the medication does not run on to the label.

9. After pouring the drug, place the cup on a flat surface and recheck the level.

10. Give the medicine cup to the patient and have the patient drink it.

After Administering the Drug

11. Wash your hands.

12. Give the patient written and oral information about the drug and answer any questions.

13. Document the date, time, drug name, dosage, expiration date, lot number, manufacturer, route, site, significant patient reactions, and patient education in the chart.

Administering and removing transdermal medications

Critical Procedure Steps

1. Identify the patient, wash your hands, and put on gloves.

2. Select the ordered transdermal patch.

3. Check the 7 Rights.

4. If you are unfamiliar with the drug, check the PDR, read the package insert, or speak with the physician.

5. Perform calculations needed to provide the prescribed dose.

6. Ask the patient about any drug allergies.

Applying the Patch

7. Remove the patch from its pouch and peel off the plastic backing.

8. Demonstrate to the patient how to remove the plastic backing.

9. Apply the patch to a reasonably hair-free site.

10. Instruct the patient how to apply the patch.

11. Avoid using extremities below the knee or elbow, skin folds, scar tissue, or burned areas.

Removing the Patch

12. Gently lift and slowly peel the patch back from the skin.

13. Wash the area with soap and dry it with a towel.

14. Explain to the patient that the area may be warm and red but that the redness will disappear.

15. Apply lotion to the area if it feels dry.

16. Instruct the patient to advise the physician if the redness doesn't go away or if a rash appears.

17. Never apply a patch to a site that was just used.

continued

After Applying or Removing the Patch

18. Wash your hands and instruct the patient to do so after applying or removing a patch.

19. Give the patient written and oral information about the drug and answer any questions.

20. Document the date, time, drug name, dosage, expiration date, lot number, manufacturer, route, site, significant patient reactions, and patient education in the chart.

Choosing Needle Sizes

Type of Injection	Needle Gauge	Needle Length
Intradermal	25–26 gauge	$\frac{3}{8}-\frac{1}{2}$ inch
Subcutaneous	23–27 gauge	$\frac{1}{2}-\frac{3}{4}$ inch
Intramuscular	18–23 gauge	1–3 inches

Choosing Syringes

- Choose the correct syringe based on the type of medication and the volume administered.
- Insulin syringes are calibrated in units

Conversion Charts for Measurements

Metric to apothecary

Volume

- 30 mL = 1 fluidounce
- 500 mL = 1 pint

- 1000 mL = 1 quart

Weight

- 0.06 g = 1 grain
- 0.5 g = 7 ¾ gr
- 1 g = 15 gr
- 4 g = 1 dram
- 30 g = 1 ounce

Metric to metric

Volume

- 0.001 L = 1 milliliter
- 0.01 L = 1 centiliter
- 0.1 L = 1 deciliter
- 1 L = 1000 mL
- 10 L = 1 dekaliter
- 100 L = 1 hectoliter
- 1000 L = 1 kiloliter

Weight

- 0.001 g = 1 mg
- 0.01 g = 1 centigram
- 0.1 g = 1 decigram
- 1 g = 1000 mg
- 10 g = 1 dekagram
- 100 g = 1 hectogram
- 1000 g = 1 kilogram

Standard to standard

Volume

- 60 drops = 1 tsp

- 3 tsp = 1 tbsp
- 6 tsp = 1 oz
- 2 tbsp = 1 oz
- 8 oz = 1 c
- 2 c = 1 pt
- 4 c = 1 qt

Drawing a Drug from an Ampule

Critical Procedure Steps

1. Identify your patient, wash your hands, and put on gloves.
2. Gently tap the top of the ampule to settle the liquid to the bottom of the ampule.
3. Wipe the ampule's neck with an alcohol swab.
4. Wrap a 2 × 2 gauze pad around the ampule's neck and snap the neck away from you.
5. Insert the filtered needle into the ampule without touching the side of the ampule.
6. Pull back on the plunger to aspirate the liquid completely into the syringe.
7. Replace with the regular needle and push the plunger until the medication just reaches the tip of the needle.

Drug Calculation Formulas

Basic formula

$$\frac{\text{desired dose}}{\text{dose on hand}} \times \text{quantity of dose on hand}$$

By weight

1. Convert the patient's weight to kilogram using either the fraction or ratio method. For accuracy when converting, round to the nearest hundredths (two decimal places).

   Fraction Method:

   a. Set up the equation. (Recall 1 lb = 2.2 kg)

   $$\frac{34 \text{ lbs}}{x} = \frac{1 \text{ lb}}{2.2 \text{ kg}}$$

   b. Cross multiply. Remember to multiply the bottom left number by the top right number and multiply the top left number by the bottom right number:

   $$x \times 1 \text{ lb} = 34 \text{ lbs} \times 2.2 \text{ kg}$$

   c. Solve for x

   $$x = 74.8 \text{ kg}$$

2. Calculate the desired dose (D) for 24 hours by multiplying the dose ordered by the weight in kilograms.

   $$8 \text{ mg} \times 74.8 \text{ kg} = \text{desired dose (D)}$$
   $$598.4 \text{ mg} = D$$

3. Calculate the desired dose (D) for one dose by dividing the amount to be received by the number of times the medication will be received in 24 hours.

   In this case, the medication is to be given four times in 24 hours.

   $$598.4 \text{ mg divided by } 4 = 149.6 \text{ mg}$$

Fraction method

1. Set up the first fraction with the dose ordered and the unknown number of capsules:

   $$\frac{30 \text{ mg}}{x}$$

2. Set up the second fraction with the amount of drug in a capsule and a single capsule:

$$\frac{10 \text{ mg}}{1 \text{ cap}}$$

3. Then use both fractions in a proportion: =

$$\frac{30 \text{ mg}}{x} = \frac{10 \text{ mg}}{1 \text{ cap}}$$

4. Cross multiply. Remember to multiply the bottom left number by the top right number and multiply the top left number by the bottom right number:

$$x \times 10 \text{ mg} = 30 \text{ mg} \times 1 \text{ cap}$$

5. To solve for x, divide both sides of the equation by 10 mg, then do the arithmetic, canceling out like terms in the top and bottom of each fraction:

$$\frac{x \times \cancel{10 \text{ mg}}}{\cancel{10 \text{ mg}}} = \frac{30 \cancel{\text{ mg}} \times 1 \text{ cap}}{10 \cancel{\text{ mg}}}$$

$$x = \frac{30 \text{ caps}}{10}$$

6. $x = 3$ caps

Ratio method

1. Set up a ratio with the unknown number of tablets and the amount of the drug ordered:

$$x : 500 \text{ mg}$$

2. Next set up a ratio with a single tablet and the amount of drug in a single tablet:

$$1 \text{ tab} : 250 \text{ mg}$$

3. Now put both of these ratios in a proportion:

$$x : 500 \text{ mg} :: 1 \text{ tab} : 250 \text{ mg}$$

4. Multiply the outer and then the inner parts of the proportion:

$$x \times 250 \text{ mg} = 500 \text{ mg} \times 1 \text{ tab}$$

5. To solve for x, divide both sides of the equation by 250 mg, then do the arithmetic, canceling out like terms in the top and bottom of each fraction:

$$\frac{x \times \cancel{250 \text{ mg}}}{\cancel{250 \text{ mg}}} = \frac{500 \cancel{\text{ mg}} \times 1 \text{ tab}}{250 \text{ mg}}$$

$$x = \frac{500 \text{ tab}}{250}$$

6. $x = 2$ tabs

Drug Categories

Category	Drug Action
Analgesic	Relieves mild to severe pain
Anesthetic	Prevents sensation of pain
Antacid/Antiulcer	Neutralizes stomach acid
Anthelmintic	Kills, paralyzes, or inhibits the growth of parasitic worms
Antiarrhythmic	Normalizes heartbeat

continued

Category	Drug Action
Antibiotics (Anti-Infectives)	Kills microorganisms or inhibits or prevents their growth
Anticholinergic	Blocks parasympathetic nerve impulses
Anticoagulant	Prevents blood clotting
Anticonvulsant	Relieves or controls seizures

Antidepressant
  Tricyclic
  MAO inhibitors
  SSRIs
	Relieves depression

Antidiabetic	Treats diabetes by reducing glucose
Antidiarrheal	Relieve diarrhea
Antidote	Counteracts action of specific drug class
Antiemetic	Prevents or relieves nausea and vomiting
Antifungal	Kills or inhibits growth of fungi
Antihistamine	Counteracts effects of histamine and relieves allergic symptoms
Antihypertensive	Reduces blood pressure
Anti-inflammatory nonsteroidal drugs	Reduces inflammation

Category	Drug Action
Antilipidemic	Lowers blood lipids
Antineoplastic	Poisons cancerous cells
Antipsychotic	Controls psychotic symptoms
Antipyretic	Reduces fever
Antiseptic	Inhibits growth of microorganisms
Antitussive	Inhibits cough reflex
Bronchodilator	Dilates bronchi
Cathartic	Induces defecation, alleviates constipation
Contraceptive	Reduces risk of pregnancy
Decongestant	Relieves nasal swelling and congestion
Diuretic	Increases urine output, reduces blood pressure and cardiac output
Expectorant	Liquefies mucus in bronchi, allows expectoration of sputum, mucus, and phlegm
Hemostatic	Controls or stops bleeding by promoting coagulation
Hormone replacement	Replaces or resolves hormone deficiency

continued

Category	Drug Action
Hypnotic or sedative	Induces sleep or relaxation
Muscle relaxant	Relaxes skeletal muscles
Mydriatic	Constricts vessels of eye or nasal passage, raises blood pressure, dilates pupil of eye in ophthalmic preparations
Stimulant (CNS)	Increases activity of brain and other organs, decreases appetite
Vasoconstrictor	Constricts blood vessels, increases blood pressure
Vasodilator	Dilates blood vessels, decreases blood pressure

Inhalation Therapy

Critical Procedure Steps

1. Identify the patient and wash your hands.
2. Check the 7 Rights.
3. Check the package insert and prepare the medication as directed.
4. Shake the container as directed and share this information with the patient.

Nasal Inhaler

5. Have the patient blow his nose.

6. Ask him to tilt his head back slightly and insert the tip of the inhaler in the nose ½ inch.

7. Point the tip straight up toward the inner corner of the eye.

8. Use the opposite hand to block the other nostril.

9. Inhale gently while quickly and firmly squeezing the inhaler.

10. Remove the inhaler tip and breathe through the mouth.

11. Shake the inhaler and repeat the process for the other nostril.

12. If indicated in the package insert, have the patient keep his head tilted back and ask him not to blow his nose for several minutes.

Oral Inhaler

5. Warm the canister by rolling it in the palms of your hands.

6. Assemble the inhaler as directed in the package insert.

7. Have the patient hold his mouth open and place the inhaler as instructed in the package insert.

8. Ask the patient to exhale normally and inhale through the canister as he depresses it.

9. The patient must be inhaling when the canister is depressed.

continued

10. Instruct the patient to breathe in until his lungs are full and hold his breath for 10 seconds.

11. Have the patient breathe out normally.

12. Repeat the process if additional "puffs" are prescribed.

After Giving an Inhalation Medication

13. Remain with the patient to monitor for changes and possible adverse reactions.

14. Recap and secure the medication container.

15. Instruct the patient in this procedure.

16. Wash your hands.

17. Give the patient an information sheet about the drug.

18. Discuss the information with the patient and answer any questions.

19. Document the date, time, drug name, dosage, expiration date, lot number, manufacturer, route, site, significant patient reactions, and patient education in the chart.

Injection Sites

Intradermal

- Administer in the upper layers of the skin.
- Common sites are the forearm and the back.
- Avoid scarred, blemished, or hairy areas.

Intramuscular

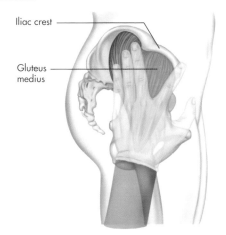

Iliac crest

Gluteus medius

A

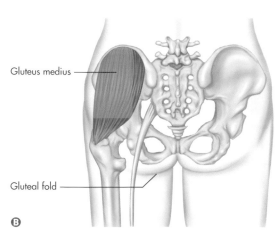

Gluteus medius

Gluteal fold

B

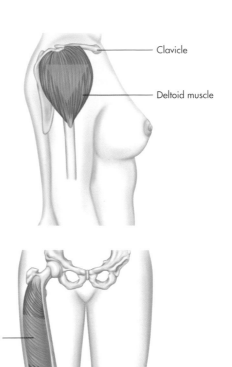

Clavicle

Deltoid muscle

Vastus lateralis
(mid-portion)

C

D

Subcutaneous

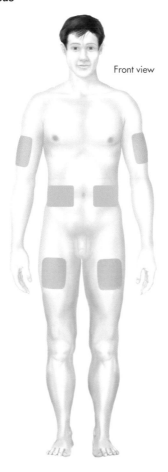

Front view

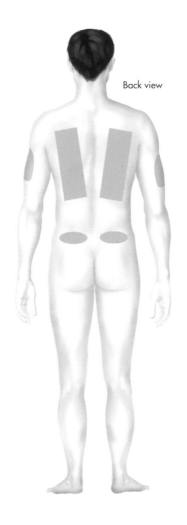

Back view

Injection Techniques

Intradermal

Critical Procedure Steps

1. Identify the patient.
2. Wash your hands and put on gloves.
3. Check the 7 Rights against the physician's order.
4. Identify the injection site, usually the forearm.
5. Prepare the skin with an alcohol swab, moving in a circle from the center out.
6. Let the skin dry before giving the injection.
7. Hold the patient's forearm and stretch the skin tight with one hand.
8. Place the needle, bevel up, almost flat against the skin and insert the needle.
9. Inject the drug gently and slowly until a wheal is raised.
10. After the full dose of the drug has been injected, withdraw the needle.
11. Properly dispose of the used materials and the needle and syringe immediately.
12. Remove the gloves and wash your hands.
13. Stay with the patient to monitor for unexpected reactions.
14. Document the injection with the date, time, drug name, dosage, expiration date, lot number, manufacturer, route, site, significant patient reactions, and any patient education in the patient's chart.

Intramuscular

Critical Procedure Steps

1. Identify the patient.
2. Wash your hands and put on gloves.
3. Check the 7 Rights against the drug order.
4. Prepare the drug and draw up the amount ordered.
5. Choose a site and gently tap it.
6. Prepare the skin with an alcohol swab, moving in a circle from the center out.
7. Let the skin dry before giving the injection.
8. Stretch the skin taut over the injection site.
9. Insert the needle with a quick, dart-like thrust at a 90-degree angle.
10. Release the skin and aspirate to check needle placement.
11. Slowly inject the drug if the needle is placed correctly (no blood appears when you aspirate).
12. After injecting the full dose of the drug, place a 2 × 2 piece of gauze over the injection site.
13. Quickly remove the needle at a 90-degree angle.
14. Use the 2 × 2 piece of gauze to apply pressure to the site and massage it, if indicated.
15. Properly dispose of used materials and the needle and syringe.

16. Remove the gloves and wash your hands.

17. Stay with the patient to monitor unexpected reactions.

18. Document the injection with the date, time, drug name, dosage, expiration date, lot number, manufacturer, route, site, significant patient reactions, and any patient education in the patient's chart.

Subcutaneous

Critical Procedure Steps

1. Identify the patient.

2. Wash your hands and put on gloves.

3. Check the 7 Rights against the drug order.

4. Prepare the drug and draw up the amount ordered.

5. Choose a site.

6. Prepare the skin with an alcohol swab, moving in a circle from the center out.

7. Let the skin dry before giving the injection.

8. Pinch the skin firmly to lift the subcutaneous tissue.

9. Position the needle, bevel up, at a 45-degree angle to the skin.

10. Insert the needle with one quick motion and release the skin.

continued

11. Inject the drug slowly.

12. After injecting the full dose of the drug, place a 2 × 2 piece of gauze over the injection site and withdraw the needle.

13. Apply pressure at the puncture site with the gauze.

14. Massage the site gently, if indicated.

15. Properly dispose of used materials and the needle and syringe.

16. Remove the gloves and wash your hands.

17. Stay with the patient to monitor unexpected reactions.

18. Document the injection with the date, time, drug name, dosage, expiration date, lot number, manufacturer, route, site.

Pediatric Patients

Giving injections

- Distract the child by talking to him or her.
- Praise the child.
- Use a topical anesthetic.
- Be swift.
- Avoid letting the child see the syringe.

Oral medication guidelines

YOU SHOULD KNOW

- Use a calibrated dropper or spoon device to measure the amount ordered.

- Administer the medication to the side of the tongue.

- Hold the child until you are sure the medication is swallowed.

- If a small amount dribbles out, do not give additional medication.

- If the child vomits within 5 minutes and you can see the medication in the vomitus, administer more medication. If you are unsure, consult the physician.

- If the medication only comes in tablet form, check a drug reference to see if it can be crushed and given with food.

Pregnancy Drug Risk Categories

Category	Description
A	*Controlled studies show no risk.* Adequate, well-controlled studies in pregnant women have not shown an increased risk of fetal abnormalities.
B	*No evidence of risk in humans.* Either animal findings show risk while human findings do not, or, if no adequate human studies have been done, animal findings are negative.
C	*Risk cannot be ruled out.* Human studies are lacking, and animal finding are either positive for fetal risk or lacking as well. Potential benefits may outweigh the risks.

continued

Category	Description
D	*Positive evidence of risk.* Studies in pregnant women, either adequate and well-controlled or observational, in pregnant women have demonstrated a risk to the fetus. Potential benefits may outweigh the risks.
X	*Contraindicated in pregnancy.* Studies in animals or pregnant women, either adequate and well-controlled or observational, have demonstrated positive evidence of fetal abnormalities.
NR	*No rating is available*

Reconstituting and Drawing a Drug

Critical Procedure Steps

1. Identify your patient, wash your hands, and put on gloves.
2. Place the drug vial and the diluent on the countertop. Wipe each with an alcohol swab.
3. Using a syringe and needle, pull the plunger back on the syringe to the amount of diluent needed to reconstitute the drug ordered.
4. Puncture the diluent vial and inject the air into the diluent.
5. Invert the vial and aspirate the diluent.

6. Remove the needle from the diluent, inject the diluent into the drug vial, and withdraw the needle

7. Properly dispose of the needle and syringe.

8. Roll the vial between your hands to mix it thoroughly.

9. Do not shake the vial unless directed to do so on the product label.

10. Prepare the second syringe and needle.

11. Pull back the plunger to the mark that reflects the amount of drug ordered.

12. Inject the air into the drug vial.

13. Invert the vial and aspirate the proper amount of drug into the syringe.

Rules for Drug Administration

YOU SHOULD KNOW

- Give only the medication the physician prescribes.
- Wash your hands before you handle the medication.
- Calculate the dose if necessary.
- Avoid leaving a prepared drug unattended.
- Never administer a drug that someone else has prepared.
- Ensure correct patient identification.

continued

- Ask the patient about drug allergies.
- Be sure the physician is in the office when you administer a drug or vaccine.
- Have the patient remain in the facility for 10 to 20 minutes after administering the drug.
- Give the patient information about the drug and its side effects.
- If the patient refuses to take the drug, discard it according to office policy.
- Do not flush it down the toilet or return it to its original container.
- Document the refusal and alert the physician.
- If you make an error in drug administration, tell the physician immediately.
- Document the drug and dose administered.
- Never document administration before giving the medication.

Top 25 Drugs by Category

Category of Pharmacologic Activity	Generic
Analgesic	Hydrocodone/ Acetaminophen
	Propoxyphene-N/Acetaminophen
Antianxiety	Alprazolam

Category of Pharmacologic Activity	Generic
Antiasthmatic	Montelukast sodium
Antibiotic	Amoxicillin
	Azithromycin
	Cephalexin
Antidepressant	Sertraline Hydrochloride
	Escitalopram Oxalate
Antidiabetic	Metformin Hydrochloride
Antihypertensive	Lisinopril
	Atenolol
	Metoprolol succinate
	Amlodipine Besylate
Antiulcer	Esomeprazole Magnesium
Bronchodilator	Albuterol Aerosol
Diuretic	Hydrochlorothiazide (HCTZ)
	Furosemide
Diuretic/Antihypertensive	Triamterenew/Hctz
Hypnotic	Zolpidem
Non-steroidal anti-inflammatory agent (NSAID)	Ibuprofen

continued

Category of Pharmacologic Activity	Generic
Statin	Atorvastatin Calcium
	Simvastatin
Steroid	Prednisone
Thyroid Hormone	Levothyroxine

Source: Adapted from "The Top 300 Prescriptions for 2005 by Number of US Prescriptions Dispensed," Rx List: The Internet Drug Index, www.rxlist.com

Z-Track Injections

Used for medications that might irritate the skin

- Pull the skin to one side.
- Insert the needle.
- Inject the medication.
- Release the skin to close off the injection site.
- Do not massage the site.

Minor Surgery

Assisting as a Floater

Critical Procedure Steps

1. Perform routine hand washing and put on exam gloves.
2. Monitor the patient during the procedure; record the results in the patient's chart.
3. During the surgery assist as needed.

4. Add sterile items to the tray as necessary.
5. Pour sterile solution into a sterile bowl as needed.
6. Assist in administering additional anesthetic.
   a. Check the medication vial two times.
   b. Clean the rubber stopper with an alcohol pad (write the date opened when using a new bottle); leave pad on top.
   c. Present the needle and syringe to the doctor.
   d. Remove the alcohol pad from the vial, and show the label to the doctor.
   e. Hold the vial upside down, and grasp the lower edge firmly; brace your wrist with your free hand.

Rationale
This firmly supports the vial to sustain the force of the needle being inserted into the rubber stopper.
   f. Allow the doctor to fill the syringe.
   g. Check the medication vial a final time

Receive specimens for laboratory examination.
   a. Uncap the specimen container; present it to the doctor for the introduction of the specimen.
   b. Replace the cap and label the container.
   c. Treat all specimens as infectious.
   d. Place the specimen container in a transport bag or other container.
   e. Complete the requisition form to send the specimen to the laboratory.

Assisting as a Sterile Scrub Assistant

Critical Procedure Steps

1. Perform a surgical scrub and put on sterile gloves.

2. Remember to remove the sterile towel covering the sterile field and instruments before gloving.

3. Close and arrange the surgical instruments on the tray.

4. Prepare for swabbing by inserting gauze squares into the sterile dressing forceps.

5. Pass the instruments as necessary.

6. Swab the wound as requested.

7. Retract the wound as requested.

8. Cut the sutures as requested.

Assisting After Minor Surgery

Critical Procedure Steps

1. Monitor the patient.

2. Put on clean exam gloves, and clean the wound with antiseptic.

3. Dress the wound.

4. Remove the gloves and wash your hands.

5. Give the patient oral postoperative instructions in addition to the release packet.

6. Discharge the patient.

7. Put on clean exam gloves.

8. Properly dispose of used materials and disposable instruments.

9. Sanitize reusable instruments and prepare them for disinfection and/or sterilization as needed.

10. Clean equipment and the exam room according to OSHA guidelines.

11. Remove the gloves and wash your hands.

Basic Instruments

Cutting and dissecting

- **Curettes**—used for scraping tissue, come in a variety of shapes and sizes, and consist of a circular blade (loop) attached to a rod-shaped handle
- **Scalpels**—consist of a handle that holds a disposable blade; specific use determines the shape and size of the blade
- **Scissors**—may be straight or curved and have either blunt or pointed tips

Grasping and clamping instruments

- **Forceps**—used to grasp or hold objects; include thumb, tissue, and sponge forceps
- **Hemostats**—used to close off blood vessels; the handles lock on ratchets, holding the jaws securely closed

- **Towel clamps**—keep towels in place during a surgical procedure to help maintain a sterile field

Retracting, dilating, and probing instruments

- **Dilators**—slender, pointed instruments; used to enlarge a body opening, such as a tear duct
- **Probes**—a slender rod with a blunt tip shaped like a bulb; used to explore wounds or body cavities and to locate or clear blockages
- **Retractors**—allow greater access to and a better view of a surgical site; may be held open by hand or have ratchets or locks to keep them open

Suturing instruments

- **Needle holders**—special instrument to hold, insert, and retrieve suture needles
- **Suture needles**—carry suture material through the tissue being sutured; may be pointed or blunt at one end; straight or curved

Creating a Sterile Field

Critical Procedure Steps

1. Clean and disinfect the Mayo stand.
2. Wash your hands and assemble the necessary materials.
3. Check the label on the instrument pack to make sure it is the correct pack for the procedure.

4. Check the date and sterilization indicator on the instrument pack to make sure the pack is still sterile.

5. Place the sterile pack on the tray or stand, and unfold the outermost fold away from yourself.

6. Unfold the sides of the pack outward, touching only the areas that will become the underside of the sterile field.

7. Open the final flap toward yourself, stepping back and away from the sterile field.

8. Place additional packaged sterile items on the sterile field.

8a. Ensure that you have the correct item or instrument and that the package is still sterile.

8b. Stand away from the sterile field.

8c. Grasp the package flaps and pull apart about halfway.

8d. Bring the corners of the wrapping beneath the package, paying attention not to contaminate the inner package or item.

8e. Hold the package over the sterile field with the opening down; with a quick movement, pull the flap completely open and snap the sterile item onto the field.

9. Place basins and bowls near the edge of the sterile field so you can pour liquids without reaching over the field.

continued

10. Use sterile transfer forceps if necessary to add additional items to the sterile field.

11. If necessary, don sterile gloves after a sterile scrub to arrange items on the sterile field.

Donning Sterile Gloves

Critical Procedure Steps

1. Obtain the correct size gloves.
2. Check the package for tears, and ensure that the expiration date has not passed.
3. Perform a surgical scrub.
4. Peel the outer wrap from gloves and place the inner wrapper on a clean surface above waist level.
5. Position gloves so the cuff end is closest to your body.
6. Touch only the flaps as you open the package.
7. Use instructions provided on inner package, if available.
8. Do not reach over the sterile inside of the inner package.
9. Follow these steps if there are no instructions:
   a. Open the package so the first flap is opened away from you.
   b. Pinch the corner and pull to one side.

    c. Put your fingertips under the side flaps and gently pull until the package is completely open.

10. Use your nondominant hand to grasp the inside cuff of the opposite glove without touching the outside of the glove.

11. Holding the glove at arm's length and waist level, insert the dominant hand into the glove with the palm facing up. Don't let the outside of the glove touch any other surface.

12. With your sterile gloved hand, slip the gloved fingers into the cuff of the other glove.

13. Pick up the other glove, touching only the outside. Don't touch any other surfaces.

14. Pull the glove up and onto your hand. Ensure that the sterile gloved hand does not touch skin.

15. Adjust your fingers as necessary, touching only glove to glove.

16. Do not adjust the cuffs because your forearms may contaminate the gloves.

17. Keep your hands in front of you, between your shoulders and waist. If you move your hands out of this area, they are considered contaminated.

18. If contamination or the possibility of contamination occurs, change gloves.

19. Remove gloves the same way you remove clean gloves, by touching only the inside.

Rules for Setting Up Trays

A sterile field is considered contaminated and must be redone if:

- An unsterile item touches the field
- Someone reaches across the field
- The field becomes wet
- The field is left unattended and uncovered
- You turn your back on the field

Rules for Sterile Technique

1. The contact of a sterile area or article with a nonsterile article renders it nonsterile.

2. If there is a doubt about the sterility of an article or area, it is considered nonsterile.

3. Unused, opened sterile supplies must be discarded or resterilized.

4. Packages are wrapped or sealed in such a way that they can be opened without contamination.

5. The edges of wrappers (1-inch margin) covering sterile supplies, the outer lips of bottles, or flasks containing sterile solutions are not considered sterile.

6. When a sterile surface or package becomes wet, it is considered contaminated.

7. Reaching over a sterile field when you are not wearing sterile clothing contaminates the area.

8. When wearing sterile gloves, keep your hands between your shoulders and your waist to maintain sterility.

9. Even in a sterile gown, your back is considered contaminated; do not turn your back on a sterile field.

Performing a Surgical Scrub

Critical Procedure Steps

1. Remove all jewelry and roll up your sleeves to above the elbow.

2. Assemble the necessary materials.

3. Turn on the faucet using the foot or knee pedal.

4. Wet your hands from the fingertips to the elbows. You must keep your hands higher than your elbows.

5. Under running water, use a sterile brush to clean under your fingernails.

6. Apply surgical soap, and scrub your hands, fingers, areas between the fingers, wrists, and forearms with the scrub sponge, using a firm

continued

circular motion. Follow the manufacturer's recommendations to determine appropriate length of time, usually 2–6 minutes.

7. Rinse from fingers to elbows, always keeping your hands higher than your elbows.

8. Thoroughly dry your hands and forearms with sterile towels, working from the hands to the elbows.

9. Turn off the faucet with the foot or knee pedal. Use a clean paper towel if a foot or knee pedal is not used.

Suture Removal

Critical Procedure Steps

1. Clean and disinfect the tray or Mayo stand.

2. Wash your hands and assemble the necessary materials.

3. Check the date and sterilization indicator on the suture removal pack.

4. Unwrap the suture removal pack, and place it on the tray or stand to create a sterile field.

5. Unwrap the sterile bowls and add them to the sterile field.

6. Pour a small amount of antiseptic solution into one bowl, and pour a small amount of hydrogen peroxide into the other bowl.

7. Cover the tray with a sterile towel to protect the sterile field while you are out of the room.

8. Escort the patient to the exam room and explain the procedure.

9. Perform a routine hand wash, remove the towel from the tray, and put on exam gloves.

10. Remove the old dressing.
    a. Lift the tape toward the middle of the dressing to avoid pulling on the wound.
    b. If the dressing adheres to the wound, cover the dressing with gauze squares soaked in hydrogen peroxide. Leave the wet gauze in place for several seconds to loosen the dressing.
    c. Save the old dressing for the doctor to inspect.

11. Inspect the wound for signs of infection.

12. Clean the wound with gauze pads soaked in antiseptic, and pat it dry with clean gauze pads.

13. Remove the gloves and wash your hands.

14. Notify the doctor that the wound is ready for examination.

15. Once the doctor indicates that the wound is sufficiently healed to proceed, put on clean exam gloves.

16. Place a square of gauze next to the wound for collecting the sutures as they are removed.

continued

17. Grasp the first suture knot with forceps.

18. Gently lift the knot away from the skin to allow room for the suture scissors.

19. Slide the suture scissors under the suture material, and cut the suture where it enters the skin

20. Gently lift the knot up and toward the wound to remove the suture without opening the wound

21. Place the suture on the gauze pad, and inspect to ensure that the entire suture is present.

22. Repeat the removal process until all sutures have been removed.

23. Count the sutures and compare the number with the number indicated in the patient's record.

24. Clean the wound with antiseptic, and allow the wound to air-dry.

25. Dress the wound as ordered, or notify the doctor if the sterile strips or butterfly closures are to be applied.

26. Observe the patient for signs of distress, such as wincing or grimacing.

27. Properly dispose of used materials and disposable instruments.

28. Remove the gloves and wash your hands.

29. Instruct the patient on wound care.

30. In the patient's chart, record pertinent information, such as the condition of the wound and the type of closures used, if any.

31. Escort the patient to the checkout area.

32. Put on clean gloves.

33. Sanitize reusable instruments and prepare them for disinfection and/or sterilization as needed.

34. Clean the equipment and exam room according to OSHA guidelines.

35. Remove the gloves and wash your hands.

Wounds

Care—Promoting healing

- Clean debris from nonsurgical wounds
- Keep the wound dry
- Sutured wounds heal more quickly
- Clean a wound daily with a mild antiseptic or soap and water
- Use an antibiotic ointment if indicated

Indications for physician's care

Patients with any of the following should seek the care of a physician:

- Jagged or gaping edges
- A face wound
- Limited movement in the area of the wound
- Tenderness or inflammation at the wound site
- Purulent drainage
- A fever greater than 100°F
- Red streaks near the wound

- A puncture wound
- Bleeding that does not stop after 10 minutes of pressure
- Sutures coming out on their own or too early

Wrapping Surgical Instruments

Critical Procedure Steps

1. Wash your hands and put on gloves before beginning to wrap the items to be sterilized.

2. Place a square of paper or muslin on the table with one point toward you. With muslin, use a double thickness. The paper or fabric must be large enough to allow all four points to cover the instruments or equipment you will be wrapping. It must also be large enough to provide an overlap, which will be used as a handling flap.

3. Place each item to be included in the pack in the center area of the paper or fabric "diamond." Items that will be used together should be wrapped together. Take care, however, that surfaces of the items do not touch each other inside the pack. Inspect each item to make sure it is operating correctly. Place hinged instruments in the pack in the open position. Wrap a small piece of paper, muslin, or gauze around delicate edges or points to protect against damage to other instruments or to the pack wrapping.

4. Place a sterilization indicator inside the pack with the instruments. Position the indicator correctly, following the manufacturer's guidelines.

5. Fold the bottom point of the diamond up and over the instruments in to the center. Fold back a small portion of the point.

6. Fold the right point of the diamond in to the center. Again, fold back a small portion of the point to be used as a handle.

7. Fold the left point of the diamond in to the center, folding back a small portion to form a handle. The pack should now resemble an open envelope.

8. Grasp the covered instruments (the bottom of the envelope) and fold this portion up, toward the top point. Fold the top point down over the pack, making sure the pack is snug but not too tight.

9. Secure the pack with autoclave tape. A "quick-opening tab" can be created by folding a small portion of the tape back onto itself. The pack must be snug enough to prevent instruments from slipping out of the wrapping or damaging each other inside the pack but loose enough to allow adequate circulation of steam through the pack.

10. Label the pack with your initials and the date. List the contents of the pack as well. If

continued

the pack contains syringes, be sure to identify the syringe size(s).

11. Place the pack aside for loading into the autoclave.

12. Remove gloves, dispose of them in the appropriate waste container, and wash your hands.

For wrapping instruments and equipment in bags or envelopes:

1. Wash your hands and put on gloves before beginning to wrap the items to be sterilized.

2. Insert the items into the bag or envelope as indicated by the manufacturer's directions. Hinged instruments should be opened before insertion into the package.

3. Close and seal the pack. Make sure the sterilization indicator is not damaged or already exposed.

4. Label the pack with your initials and the date. List the contents of the pack as well. The pens or pencils used to label the pack must be waterproof; otherwise, the contents of the pack and date of sterilization will be obliterated.

5. Place the pack aside for loading into the autoclave.

6. Remove gloves, dispose of them in the appropriate waste container, and wash your hands.

Nutrition

Alerting Patients with Food Allergies to the Dangers of Common Foods

Critical Procedure Steps

1. Identify the patient and introduce yourself.

2. Discuss the results of the patient's allergy tests (if available), reinforcing the physician's instructions. List the foods the patient has been found to be allergic to. Provide the patient with a checklist of those foods.

3. Discuss with the patient the possible allergic reactions those foods can cause.

4. Talk about how the patient can avoid or eliminate those foods from the diet. Point out that the patient needs to be alert to avoid the allergy-causing foods not only in their basic forms but also as ingredients in prepared dishes and packaged foods. (Patients allergic to peanuts, for example, should avoid products containing peanut oil as well as peanuts.) Tell the patient to read labels carefully and to inquire at restaurants about the use of those ingredients in dishes listed on the menu.

5. With the physician's or dietitian's consent, talk with the patient about the possibility of finding adequate substitutes for the foods if they are among the patient's favorites. Also discuss,

continued

if necessary, how the patient can obtain the nutrients in those foods from other sources (for example, the need for extra calcium sources if the patient is allergic to dairy products). Provide these explanations to the patient in writing, if appropriate, along with supplementary materials such as recipe pamphlets, a list of resources for obtaining food substitutes, and so on.

6. Discuss with the patient the procedures to follow if the allergy-causing foods are accidentally ingested.

7. Answer the patient's questions and remind the patient that you and the rest of the medical team are available if any questions or problems arise later on.

8. Document the patient education session or interchange in the patient's chart, indicate the patient's understanding, and initial the entry.

Calories Burned During Activities

Activity	120-lb Person	190-lb Person
Bicycling	360	570
Football (touch)	288	456
Calisthenics	324	516
Handball	456	720
Hiking	300	480
Running (10 mph)	720	1140

Activity	120-lb Person	190-lb Person
Skiing (downhill)	426	672
Skiing (cross-country)	564	888
Soccer	456	720
Swimming	228	366
Tennis	330	522
Volleyball	258	408
Walking (2 mph)	156	252

Food Label Terms

- **Low calorie**—less than or equal to 40 calories per serving
- **Reduced calorie**—at least 25% fewer calories per serving than the food it replaces
- **Cholesterol free**—less than or equal to 2 mg cholesterol per serving
- **Low cholesterol**—less than or equal to 20 mg cholesterol per serving
- **Reduced cholesterol**—at least 25% less cholesterol per serving than the food it replaces
- **Low fat**—less than or equal to 3 g fat per serving
- **Reduced fat**—at least 25% less fat per serving than the food it replaces
- **Sodium free**—less than or equal to 5 mg sodium per serving

- **Very low sodium**—less than or equal to 35 mg sodium per serving
- **Low sodium**—less than or equal to 140 mg sodium per sodium
- **Reduced sodium**—at least 25% less sodium per serving than the food it replaces

Information Sources

- American Cancer Society—(800) ACS-2345
- American Diabetes Association—(800) DIABETES
- American Dietetic Association—(800) 877-1600
- American Heart Association—(214) 373-6300
- Anorexia Nervosa and Related Eating Disorders—(847) 831-3438
- National Association of Anorexia Nervosa and Associated Disorders—(206) 282-3587
- National Eating Disorders Association—(206) 383-3587
- Overeaters Anonymous (OA)—(505) 891-2664

Saturated Fat and Cholesterol Sources

Food	Saturated Fat	Cholesterol
Cheddar cheese (1 oz)	6.0 g	30 mg
Mozzarella, part skim (1 oz)	3.1 g	15 mg
Whole milk (1 c)	5.1 g	33 mg
Skim milk (1 c)	0.3 g	4 mg

Food	Saturated Fat	Cholesterol
Butter (1 tbsp)	7.1 g	31 mg
Mayonnaise (1 tbsp)	1.7 g	8 mg
Tuna in oil (3 oz)	1.4 g	55 mg
Tuna in water (3 oz)	0.3 g	48 mg
Lean ground beef, broiled (3 oz)	6.2 g	74 mg
Leg of lamb, roasted (3 oz)	5.6 g	78 mg
Bacon (3 slices)	3.3 g	16 mg
Chicken breast, roasted (3 oz)	0.9 g	73 mg

Serving Sizes

Group	Quantity
Bread, cereal, rice, pasta	• 1 slice bread • 1 oz ready-to-eat cereal • ½ c cooked cereal, rice, or pasta
Vegetable	• 1 c raw leafy vegetables • ½ c other vegetables • ¾ c vegetable juice

continued

Group	Quantity
Fruit	• 1 medium apple, banana, or orange
	• ½ c chopped, cooked, or canned fruit
	• ¾ c fruit juice
Milk, yogurt, cheese	• 1 c milk or yogurt
	• 1½ oz natural cheese
	• 2 oz process cheese
Meat, poultry, fish, dry beans, eggs, and nuts	• 2–3 oz cooked lean meat, poultry, or fish
	• ½ c cooked dry beans or 1 egg counts as 1 oz lean meat
	• 2 tbsp peanut butter or ⅓ c nuts counts as 1 oz meat

Teaching a Patient to Read a Food Label

Critical Procedure Steps

1. Identify the patient and introduce yourself.
2. Explain that food labels can be used as a valuable source of information when planning or implementing a prescribed diet.

3. Using a label from a food package, point out the Nutrition Facts section.

4. Describe the various elements on the label.
   - Serving size is the basis for the nutrition information provided.
   - Calories and calories from fat show the proportion of fat calories in the product.
   - The % Daily Value section shows how many grams (g) or milligrams (mg) of a variety of nutrients are contained in one serving. Then the label shows the percentage (%) of the recommended daily intake of each given nutrient (assuming a diet of 2000 calories a day).
   - Recommendations for total amounts of various nutrients for both a 2000-calorie and a 2500-calorie diet are shown in chart form near the bottom of the label. These numbers provide the basis for the daily value percentages.
   - Ingredients are listed in order from largest quantity to smallest quantity.

5. Inform the patient that a variety of similar products with significantly different nutritional values are often available. Explain that patients can use nutrition labels to evaluate and compare similar products. Patients must consider what a product contributes to their diets, not simply what it lacks. To do this, patients must read the entire label.

6. Ask the patient to compare two other similar products and determine which would fit in

continued

better as part of a healthy, nutritious diet that meets that patient's individual needs.

7. Document the patient education session in the patient's chart, indicate the patient's understanding, and initial the entry.

Vitamins

Vitamin	Function
A	Production of visual receptors, mucus; normal growth for bones and teeth, epithelial tissue repair
B1	Carbohydrate metabolism
B2	Carbohydrate and fat metabolism, cell growth
B6	Protein, antibody, and nucleic acid production
B12	Myelin production, carbohydrate and nucleic acid metabolism
Biotin	Protein, fat, and nucleic acid metabolism
Folic acid	Amino acid, DNA, and red blood cell production
Pantothenic acid	Carbohydrate and fat metabolism
C	Collagen, amino acid, and hormone production; iron absorption

Vitamin	Function
D	Calcium absorption
E	Prevents breakdown of certain tissues
K	Blood clotting

Source: Reprinted courtesy of the U.S. Department of Agriculture.

Patient Education

Breast Self-Exam

Patient Education Tips

1. Explain the purpose of BSE.
2. Assist the patient to the standing position, and instruct her to use a large mirror to view the breasts during this part of the procedure.
3. Explain to the patient what she should look for when inspecting her breasts while standing.
4. Demonstrate the positioning of arms and hands for this visual inspection: first, her arms at her sides; then, her arms raised and her hands clasped behind her head; finally, her arms lowered with her hands on her hips.
5. Demonstrate, on the patient's breast, how to perform the small rotary motions with the flat pads of the fingers from the outer rim (including the armpit and collarbone area)

toward the nipple. (Synthetic breast models are available that may be helpful in teaching the proper technique.)

6. Demonstrate how to inspect the nipples.

7. Ask the patient to practice the procedure.

8. Observe the patient's self-exam technique. (If the patient is reluctant to examine herself in front of you, have her repeat the highlights of the procedure.)

9. Assist the patient to lie down, with a small pillow or folded towel under the shoulder on the side to be examined.

10. Repeat steps 5 through 8.

11. Suggest that the patient mark her calendar for a monthly reminder to perform the exam 1 week after the onset of menses.

12. Give the patient educational materials that explain how to perform BSE.

Testicular Self-Exam

Patient Education Tips

1. TSE should be performed after a warm shower or bath, when scrotal skin is relaxed.

2. The man first observes the testes for changes in appearance, such as swelling. He then manually examines each testicle, gently rolling it between the fingers and thumbs of both hands to feel for hard lumps.

3. After examining each testicle, the man should locate the area of the epididymis and spermatic cord. This area can be felt as a cordlike structure originating at the top back of each testicle.

Warning Signs of Cancer (*CAUTION*)

- **C**hange in bowel or bladder habits
- **A** sore that does not heal
- **U**nusual bleeding or discharge
- **T**hickening or lump in a breast or elsewhere
- **I**ndigestion or difficulty in swallowing
- **O**bvious change in a wart or mole
- **N**agging cough or hoarseness

Patient Instructions

Informing the Patient of Guidelines for Surgery

Critical Procedure Steps

1. Review the patient's chart to determine the type of surgery to be performed.
2. Tell the patient that you will be providing both verbal and written instructions that should be followed prior to surgery.
3. Inform the patient about policies regarding makeup, jewelry, contact lenses, wigs, dentures, and so on.

continued

4. Tell the patient to leave money and valuables at home.

5. If applicable, suggest appropriate clothing for the patient to wear for postoperative ease and comfort.

6. Explain the need for someone to drive the patient home following an outpatient surgical procedure.

7. Tell the patient the correct time to arrive in the office or at the hospital for the procedure.

8. Inform the patient of dietary restrictions. Be sure to use specific, clear instructions about what may or may not be ingested and at what time the patient must abstain from eating or drinking. Also explain these points:
   a. The reasons for the dietary restrictions
   b. The possible consequences of not following the dietary restrictions

9. Ask patients who smoke to refrain from or reduce cigarette smoking during at least the 8 hours prior to the procedure. Explain to the patient that reducing smoking improves the level of oxygen in the blood during surgery.

10. Suggest that the patient shower or bathe the morning of the procedure or the evening before.

11. Instruct the patient about medications to take or avoid before surgery.

12. If necessary, clarify any information about which the patient is unclear.

13. Provide written surgical guidelines, and suggest that the patient call the office if additional questions arise.

14. Document the instruction in the patient's chart.

Pre-Exam Instructions

- Have the patient empty his bladder or bowels. (Collect a urine specimen if it is ordered.)
- Ask the patient to disrobe according to the type of exam.
- Have the patient put on a gown and drape as indicated.

Post-Exam Instructions

- Ask the patient to dress and assist as necessary.
- Tell the patient when he might expect the results of any lab tests performed.
- Inform the patient if and when a follow-up appointment is needed.

Physical Exam

Assisting with a General PE

Critical Procedure Steps

1. Wash your hands and adhere to Standard Precautions.
2. Assemble the equipment and supplies.

continued

3. Arrange the equipment and supplies in a logical order for the physician's use.

4. Identify the patient.

5. Obtain the patient's weight and height.

6. Obtain a urine specimen before the patient undresses for the exam.

7. Explain the procedure and exam to the patient.

8. Review the patient's medical history with the patient if the office policy requires it.

9. Obtain blood specimens or other laboratory tests as ordered.

10. Obtain vital statistics per the physician's preference.

11. Provide the patient with an appropriate gown and drape, and explain where the opening for the gown is placed.

12. Obtain the EKG, if ordered.

13. Assist the patient to a sitting position at the end of the table with the drape placed across his legs.

14. Inform the physician that the patient is ready, and remain in the room to assist the physician.

15. You may be asked to shut off the light in the exam room to allow the patient's pupils to dilate for a retinal exam.

16. Hand the instruments to the physician as requested.

17. Assist the patient to the supine position for examination of the front of the body.

18. If a gynecological exam is indicated, assist and drape the patient in the lithotomy position.

19. If a rectal exam is needed, assist and drape the patient in the Sims' position.

20. Assist the patient to a prone position for a posterior body examination.

21. When the exam is complete, assist the patient into the sitting position and have them sit for a brief period of time.

22. Ask the patient if he needs assistance in dressing.

23. Properly dispose of contaminated materials.

24. Remove the table paper and pillow covering, and dispose of them in the proper container.

25. Disinfect and clean counters and the table with a disinfectant.

26. Sanitize and sterilize instruments, if needed.

27. Prepare the room for the next patient by replacing the table paper, pillow cover, equipment and supplies.

28. Document the procedure.

Assisting with a Needle Biopsy

Critical Procedure Steps

1. Identify the patient and introduce yourself; instruct the patient as needed.

continued

2. Wash your hands and assemble the necessary materials.

3. Prepare the sterile field and instruments.

4. Put on exam gloves.

5. Cleanse the biopsy site. Prepare the patient's skin.

6. Remove the gloves, wash your hands, and put on clean exam gloves.

7. Assist the doctor as she injects anesthetic.

8. During the procedure, help drape and position the patient.

9. If you will be handing the doctor the instruments, remove the gloves, perform a surgical scrub, and put on sterile gloves.

10. Place the sample in a properly labeled specimen bottle, complete the laboratory requisition form, and package the specimen for immediate transport to the laboratory.

11. Dress the patient's wound site.

12. Properly dispose of used supplies and instruments.

13. Clean and disinfect the room according to OSHA guidelines.

14. Remove the gloves and wash your hands.

Components and Materials

Component	Materials Required*
General appearance	No special materials
Head	No special materials
Neck	No special materials
Eyes and vision	Penlight, ophthalmoscope, vision and color vision charts
Ears and hearing	Otoscope, audiometer
Nose and sinuses	Penlight, nasal speculum
Mouth and throat	Gloves, tongue depressor
Chest and lungs	Stethoscope
Heart	Stethoscope
Breasts	No special materials
Abdomen	Stethoscope
Genitalia (women)	Gloves, vaginal speculum, lubricant
Genitalia (men)	Gloves
Rectum	Gloves, lubricant
Musculoskeletal system	Tape measure
Neurological system	Reflex hammer, penlight

*Gloves should always be worn if your hands will come in contact with the patient's non-intact skin, blood, and/or body fluids.

Exam Methods

Auscultation
- The process of listening to body sounds
- Used to assess sounds from the heart, lungs, and abdominal organs

Inspection
- The visualization of the patient's entire body and overall appearance
- Used to assess posture, mannerisms, hygiene, body size, shape, color, position, symmetry, and the presence of rashes or growths

Manipulation
- The systematic moving of a patient's body parts
- Used to check for abnormalities that affect movement

Mensuration
- The process of measuring
- Used to assess height and weight, growth, and extremity diameter

Palpation
- The process of using touch for assessing a patient's body parts
- Used to assess texture, temperature, shape, and the presence of vibrations or movement in underlying tissues

Percussion

- Tapping or striking the body to hear sounds or feel vibrations
- Used to determine the location, size, or density of a body structure or organ under the skin

Positions

Dorsal recumbent

- The patient lies face up, with his back supporting all his weight.
- This position is the same as the supine position, except that the patient's knees are drawn up and the feet are flat on the table.
- The physician may examine the head, neck, chest, and heart while a patient is in this position.
- The patient is normally draped from the neck or underarms down to the feet.
- Patients who have leg disabilities may find the dorsal recumbent position uncomfortable or even impossible.
- Patients who are elderly or have painful disorders such as arthritis or back pain may find the dorsal recumbent position more comfortable than the supine position because the knees are bent.
- This position is sometimes used as an alternative to the lithotomy position when patients have severe arthritis or joint deformities.

Fowler's

- The patient lies back on an examining table on which the head is elevated.

- The head of the table can be raised to a 90-degree angle; the most common position is a 45-degree angle.
- The doctor may examine the head, neck, and chest areas while the patient is in this position.
- The patient is usually draped from the neck or underarms down to the feet.
- Fowler's position is one of the best positions for examining patients who are experiencing shortness of breath or individuals with a lower-back injury.

Knee-chest

- The patient is lying on the table facedown, supporting the body with the knees and chest.
- The patient should have the thighs at a 90-degree angle to the table and slightly separated.
- The head is turned to one side, and the arms are placed to the side or above the head.
- The patient may need your assistance to assume this position correctly and to maintain it during the exam.
- The knee-chest position is used during exams of the anal and perineal areas and during certain proctologic procedures.
- Some patients—those who are pregnant, obese, or elderly—have difficulty assuming this position. An alternative that puts less strain on the patient and is easier to maintain is the knee-elbow position. This position is the same as the knee-chest position except that the patient supports body

weight with the knees and elbows rather than the knees and chest.

- In either of these two positions, the patient is commonly covered with a fenestrated drape, in which a special opening provides access to the area to be examined.

Lithotomy

- The patient lies on her back with her knees bent and her feet in stirrups attached to the end of the examining table.
- You may need to help the patient place her feet in the stirrups. She should then slide forward to position her buttocks near the edge of the table.
- Many women are embarrassed and physically uncomfortable in this position, so you should not ask a patient to remain in this position any longer than necessary.
- Use a large drape that covers the patient from the breasts to the ankles. Placing the drape with one point or corner between the legs will make the exam easier in this position.
- A patient with severe arthritis or joint deformities in the hips or knees may have difficulty assuming the lithotomy position. She may be able to place only one leg in the stirrup, or she may need your assistance in separating her thighs.
- An alternative position for such a patient is the dorsal recumbent position. Other patients who may have difficulty with the lithotomy position are those who are obese or in the late stages of pregnancy.

Proctologic

- The patient is bent at the hips at a 90-degree angle.
- The patient can assume this position by standing next to the examining table and bending at the waist until the chest rests on the table.
- If an adjustable examining table is available, the patient can assume the position by lying prone on the table, which is then raised in the middle with both ends pointing down. This places the patient at the correct 90-degree angle.
- In either variation of this position, the patient is draped with a fenestrated drape, as in the knee-chest position.

Prone

- The patient is lying flat on the table, facedown.
- The patient's head is turned to one side, and his arms are placed at his sides or bent at the elbows.
- The patient is normally draped from the upper back to the feet.
- With the patient in this position, the physician can examine the back, feet, or musculoskeletal system.
- The prone position is unsuitable for women in advanced stages of pregnancy, obese patients, patients with respiratory difficulties, or the elderly.

Sims'

- The patient lies on the left side with the left leg slightly bent, and the left arm placed behind the back so that the patient's weight is resting primarily on the chest.

- The right knee is bent and raised toward the chest, and the right arm is bent toward the head for support.
- The patient is draped from the upper back to the feet.
- Sims' position is used during anal or rectal exams and may also be used for perineal and certain pelvic exams.
- Patients with joint deformities of the hips and knees may have difficulty assuming this position.

Sitting

- The patient sits at the edge of the examining table without back support.
- The physician examines the patient's head, neck, chest, heart, back, and arms.
- While the patient is in the sitting position, the physician evaluates the patient's ability to fully expand the lungs.
- She then checks the upper body parts for symmetry, the degree to which one side is the same as the other.
- In this position the drape is placed across the patient's lap for men or across the patient's chest and lap for women.
- If a patient is too weak to sit unsupported, another position is necessary. One possible alternative is the supine position.

Supine (recumbent)

- The patient lies flat on the back.
- This is the most relaxed position for many patients.

- A doctor can examine the head, neck, chest, heart, abdomen, arms, and legs when a patient is in the supine position.
- The patient is normally draped from the neck or underarms down to the feet.
- The supine position may not be comfortable for patients who become short of breath easily. Also, patients with a back injury or lower-back pain may find it uncomfortable.
- You can make these patients more comfortable by placing a pillow under their heads and under their knees. Some patients, however, may need to be placed in the dorsal recumbent position.

Trendelenburg's

- The patient is supine on a tilted table with the head lower than the legs. Some tables have flexible positioning so that the patient's legs can be bent with the feet lower than the knees.
- Although physicians do not generally use this position for physical exams, they use it in certain surgical procedures or emergencies.
- If this position is necessary on a standard examining table, you can place the patient with the feet at the head of the table and then raise the head.
- This position may be used for a patient with low blood pressure or a patient experiencing shock.
- It cannot be used for patients who have a head injury, however.
- The drape is typically positioned from the neck or underarms down to the knees.

Positioning the Patient for an Exam

Critical Procedure Steps

1. Identify the patient and introduce yourself.

2. Wash your hands.

3. Explain the procedure to the patient.

4. Provide a gown or drape if the physician has requested one, and instruct the patient in the proper way to wear it after disrobing. Allow the patient privacy while disrobing, and assist only if the patient requests help.

5. Explain to the patient the necessary exam and the position required.

6. Ask the patient to step on the stool or the pullout step of the examining table. If necessary, assist the patient onto the examining table.

7. Assist the patient into the required position.

8. Drape the client to prevent exposure and avoid embarrassment. Place pillows for comfort as needed.

9. Adjust the drapes during the exam.

10. On completion of the exam, assist the client as necessary out of the position and provide privacy as the client dresses.

Vision Screening

Critical Procedure Steps

Distance Vision

1. Wash your hands, identify the patient, and explain the procedure.
2. Mount the eye chart at eye level.
3. Make a mark on the floor 20 feet away from the chart.
4. Have the patient stand at the 20-foot mark with her heels at the line.
5. Instruct the patient to keep both eyes open and not to squint or lean forward during the test.
6. Test the patient's eyes in order according to office policy.
7. Have the patient read the lines beginning with the 20-foot line or according to office policy.
8. Note the smallest line the patient can read or identify.
9. Record the results as a fraction.
10. Repeat the procedure for each eye.
11. Record the results for each eye.
12. Note and record any observations of squinting, head tilting, or excessive blinking or tearing.

13. Clean the occluder with a gauze square dampened with alcohol.

14. Properly dispose of the gauze square and wash your hands.

Near Vision

1. Wash your hands, identify the patient, and explain the procedure.

2. Have the patient hold the near vision card at a distance of 14 to 16 inches.

3. Have the patient keep both eyes open and read or identify the letters, symbols, or paragraphs.

4. Record the smallest line read without error.

5. Clean the card if indicated.

6. Wash your hands.

Color Vision

1. Wash your hands, identify the patient, and explain the procedure.

2. Hold one of the color charts or books at the patient's normal reading distance.

3. Ask the patient to tell you the number or symbol within the colored dots on each chart or page.

4. Proceed through all the charts or pages.

5. Record the number correctly identified and failed with a slash between them.

6. Clean the charts if indicated.

7. Wash your hands.

Pulmonary Function

Respiratory Volumes and Capacities

Test	Typical Volume
Tidal volume (TV)	500 mL
Inspiratory reserve volume (IRV)	3000 mL
Expiratory reserve volume (ERV)	1100 mL
Residual volume (RV)	1200 mL
Inspiratory capacity (IC)	3500 mL
Functional residual capacity (FRC)	2300 mL
Vital capacity (VC)	4600 mL
Total lung capacity (TLC)	5800 mL

Tests

Test	Definition
Vital capacity (VC)	Total volume of air that can be exhaled after maximum inspiration
Inspiratory capacity (IC)	Amount of air that can be inhaled after normal expiration
Functional residual capacity (FRC)	Amount of air remaining in lungs after normal expiration

Test	Definition
Total lung capacity (TLC)	Total volume of lungs when maximally inflated
Forced vital capacity (FVC)	Greatest volume of air that can be expelled when person performs rapid, forced expiratory maneuver
Forced expiratory volume (FEV)	Volume of air expelled in first, second, or third second of FVC
Peak expiratory flow rate (PEFR)	Greatest rate of flow during forced expiration
Forced expiratory flow (FEF)	Average rate of flow during middle half of FVC
Maximal voluntary ventilation (MVV)	Greatest volume of air breathed per unit of time
Tidal volume (TV)	Amount of air inhaled or exhaled during normal breathing
Minute volume (MV)	Total amount of air expired per minute
Inspiratory reserve volume (IRV)	Amount of air inspired above normal inspiration
Expiratory reserve volume (ERV)	Amount of air exhaled after normal expiration
Residual volume (RV)	Amount of air remaining in lungs after forced expiration

Vaccine Dosages

Vaccine dosages are standard and clearly labeled on the package insert. Confirm the amount administered for each vaccine by consulting the package insert.

Vital Signs and Measurements

Apical Pulse

Location

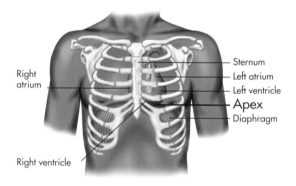

Sternum
Left atrium
Left ventricle
Apex
Diaphragm
Right atrium
Right ventricle

Blood Pressure (BP)

Taking BP in adults and older children

Critical Procedure Steps

1. Gather the equipment and make sure it is in working order and calibrated.
2. Identify the patient.

3. Wash your hands and explain the procedure.

4. Have the patient sit in a quiet area and roll up her sleeves if indicated.

5. Have the patient rest her arm on a flat surface so that the midpoint of the upper arm is at heart level.

6. Select an appropriate sized cuff.

7. Locate the brachial artery.

8. Position the cuff so that the midline of the bladder is above the arterial pulsation, one inch above the antecubital space.

9. Place the manometer at eye level so that it can be easily read.

10. Close the valve of the pressure bulb until it is finger tight.

11. Inflate the cuff rapidly to 70 mm Hg then in 10 mm Hg increments while palpating the radial pulse with your other hand.

12. Note the level of pressure where the radial pulse disappears and subsequently reappears when the pressure is released.

13. Open the valve, release the pressure completely, and wait 30 seconds.

14. Appropriately place the stethoscope earpieces in your ears, adjusting for comfort and a snug fit.

15. Place the head of the stethoscope over the brachial artery pulsation holding it firmly in place with the index and middle fingers.

continued

16. Inflate the bladder rapidly to 20 to 30 mm Hg above the palpated pressure.

17. Open the valve and slowly deflate the cuff 2 mm per second.

18. As the pressure falls, note the level of pressure where the first repetitive sounds appear (systolic pressure).

19. Continue deflating the cuff and note the point at which the sound changes from strong to muffled.

20. Continue deflating the cuff and note when the sound disappears (diastolic pressure).

21. Deflate the cuff completely and remove it from the patient's arm.

22. Record the three numbers, separated by slashes, in the patient's chart.

23. Properly store the cuff in the holder.

24. Disinfect the earpieces and diaphragm of the stethoscope with alcohol.

25. Properly dispose of any disposable supplies.

26. Wash your hands.

Taking BP of a young child

Critical Procedure Steps

1. Ideally, take the patient's blood pressure before performing other tests or procedures that

may cause anxiety. In this way you can avoid a falsely high result.

2. Be sure to use the correct cuff size for the child or infant. The bladder width should not exceed two-thirds the length of the upper or lower arm. The bladder should cover three-fourths the circumference of the extremity.

3. Do not attempt to estimate an infant's blood pressure by the palpatory method.

4. Inflate the pressure cuff to 20 mm Hg above the point at which the radial pulse disappears.

5. Deflate the cuff at a rate of 2 mm Hg per second.

6. You may continue to hear a heartbeat on a child or infant until the pressure reaches zero, so note when the strong heartbeat becomes muffled.

Conversions and Equivalents

Height

In	Cm	In	Cm	In	Cm
20	51	42	107	64	163
22	56	44	112	66	168

continued

In	Cm	In	Cm	In	Cm
24	61	46	117	68	173
26	66	48	122	70	178
28	71	50	127	72	183
30	76	52	132	74	188
32	81	54	137	76	193
34	86	56	142	78	198
36	91	58	147	80	203
38	97	60	152		
40	102	62	157		

Note: cm = in × 2.54. Conversions are rounded to nearest whole number.

Temperature

°F	°C	°F	°C	°F	°C
95.0	35.0	99.4	37.4	103.8	39.9
95.2	35.1	99.6	37.6	104.0	40.0
95.4	35.2	99.8	37.7	104.2	40.1
95.6	35.3	100.0	37.8	104.4	40.2
95.8	35.4	100.2	37.9	104.6	40.3

°F	°C	°F	°C	°F	°C
96.0	35.6	100.4	38.0	104.8	40.4
96.2	35.7	100.6	38.1	105.0	40.6
96.4	35.8	100.8	38.2	105.2	40.7
96.6	35.9	101.0	38.3	105.4	40.8
96.8	36.0	101.2	38.4	105.6	40.9
97.0	36.1	101.4	38.6	105.8	41.0
97.2	36.2	101.6	38.7	106.0	41.1
97.4	36.3	101.8	38.8	106.2	41.2
97.6	36.4	102.0	38.9	106.4	41.3
97.8	36.6	102.2	39.0	106.6	41.4
98.0	36.7	102.4	39.1	106.8	41.6
98.2	36.8	102.6	39.2	107.0	41.7
98.4	36.9	102.8	39.3	107.2	41.8
98.6	37.0	103.0	39.4	107.4	41.9
98.8	37.1	103.2	39.6	107.6	42.0
99.0	37.2	103.4	39.7	107.8	42.1
99.2	37.3	103.6	39.8	108.0	42.2

Weight

Lb	Kg	Lb	Kg	Lb	Kg
10	4.5	95	43.1	180	81.7
15	6.8	100	45.4	185	84.0
20	9.1	105	47.7	190	86.3
25	11.4	110	49.9	195	88.5
30	13.6	115	52.2	200	90.8
35	15.9	120	54.5	205	93.1
40	18.2	125	56.8	210	95.3
45	20.4	130	59.0	215	97.6
50	22.7	135	61.3	220	99.9
55	25.0	140	63.6	225	102.2
60	27.2	145	65.8	230	104.4
65	29.5	150	68.1	235	106.7
70	31.8	155	70.4	240	109.0
75	34.1	160	72.6	245	111.2
80	36.3	165	74.9	250	113.5
85	38.6	170	77.2		
90	40.9	175	79.5		

Note: kg = lb × 0.454; lb = kg × 2.205. Conversions are rounded to nearest tenth.

Measuring Height

Adults and older children

Critical Procedure Steps

1. With the patient off the scale, raise the height bar well above the patient's head and swing out the extension.

2. Ask the patient to step on the center of the scale and to stand up straight and look forward.

3. Gently lower the height bar until the extension rests on the patient's head.

4. Have the patient step off the scale before reading the measurement.

5. If the patient is fewer than 50 inches tall, read the height on the bottom part of the ruler; if the patient is more than 50 inches tall, read the height on the top movable part of the ruler at the point at which it meets the bottom part of the ruler. Note that the numbers increase on the bottom part of the bar and decrease on the top, movable part of the bar. Read the height in the right direction.

6. Record the patient's height.

7. Have the patient put her shoes back on, if necessary.

8. Properly dispose of the used towel and wash your hands.

Toddlers

Critical Procedure Steps

1. Measure the child's height in the same manner as you measure adult height, or have the child stand with his back against the height chart. Measure height at the crown of the head.

2. Record the height in the patient's chart.

3. Properly dispose of the towel (if used) and wash your hands.

Measuring Weight

Adults and older children

Critical Procedure Steps

1. Identify the patient and introduce yourself.

2. Wash your hands and explain the procedure to the patient.

3. Check to see whether the scale is in balance by moving all the weights to the left side. The indicator should be level with the middle mark. If not, check the manufacturer's directions and adjust it to ensure a zero balance. If you are using a scale equipped to measure either kilograms or pounds, check to see that it is set on the desired units and that the upper and lower weights show the same units.

4. Place a disposable towel on the scale or have the patient leave their sock on.

5. Ask the patient to remove her shoes, if that is the standard office policy.

6. Ask the patient to step on the center of the scale, facing forward. Assist as necessary.

7. Place the lower weight at the highest number that does not cause the balance indicator to drop to the bottom.

8. Move the upper weight slowly to the right until the balance bar is centered at the middle mark, adjusting as necessary.

9. Add the two weights together to get the patient's weight.

10. Record the patient's weight in the chart to the nearest quarter of a pound or tenth of a kilogram.

11. Return the weights to their starting positions on the left side.

Toddlers

Critical Procedure Steps

1. Identify the patient and obtain permission from the parent to weigh the toddler.

2. Wash your hands and explain the procedure to the parent.

continued

3. Check to see whether the scale is in balance, and place a disposable towel on the scale or have the patient wear shoes or socks, depending upon the policy of the facility.

4. Ask the parent to hold the patient and to step on the scale. Follow the procedure for obtaining the weight of an adult.

5. Have the parent put the child down or hand the child to another staff member.

6. Obtain the parent's weight.

7. Subtract the parent's weight from the combined weight to determine the weight of the child.

8. Record the patient's weight in the chart to the nearest quarter of a pound or tenth of a kilogram.

Measuring Infants

Critical Procedure Steps

Weight

1. Identify the patient and obtain permission from the parent to weigh the infant.

2. Wash your hands and explain the procedure to the parent.

3. Ask the parent to undress the infant.

4. Check to see whether the infant scale is in balance, and place a disposable towel on it.

5. Have the parent place the child face up on the scale (or on the examining table if the scale is built into it). Keep one hand over the infant at all times and hold a diaper over a male patient's penis to catch any urine the infant might void.

6. Place the lower weight at the highest number that does not cause the balance indicator to drop to the bottom.

7. Move the upper weight slowly to the right until the balance bar is centered at the middle mark, adjusting as necessary.

8. Add the two weights together to get the infant's weight.

9. Record the infant's weight in the chart in pounds and ounces or to the nearest tenth of a kilogram.

10. Return the weights to their starting positions on the left side.

Length: Scale with Length (Height) Bar

11. If the scale has a height bar, move the infant toward the head of the scale or examining table until her head touches the bar.

12. Have the parent hold the infant by the shoulders in this position.

continued

13. Holding the infant's ankles, gently extend the legs and slide the bottom bar to touch the soles of the feet.

14. Note the length and release the infant's ankles.

15. Record the length in the patient's chart.

Length: Scale or Examining Table without Length (Height) Bar

11. If neither the scale nor the examining table has a height bar, have the parent position the infant close to the head of the examining table and hold the infant by the shoulders in this position.

12. Place a stiff piece of cardboard against the crown of the infant's head, and mark a line on the towel or paper, or hold a yardstick against the cardboard.

13. Holding the infant's ankles, gently extend the legs and draw a line on the towel or paper to mark the heel, or note the measure on the yardstick.

14. Release the infant's ankles and measure the distance between the two markings on the towel or paper using the yardstick or a tape measure.

15. Record the length in the patient's chart.

Head Circumference

Measurement of head circumference may be performed at the same time as weight and length, or it may be part of the general physical exam.

16. With the infant in a sitting or supine position, place the tape measure around the infant's head at the forehead.

17. Adjust the tape so that it surrounds the infant's head at its largest circumference.

18. Overlap the ends of the tape, and read the measure at the point of overlap.

19. Remove the tape, and record the circumference in the patient's chart.

20. Properly dispose of the used towel and wash your hands.

Normal Ranges

Adults

Vital Sign	Range
Temperature	
Oral (°F)	97.6–99.6
Rectal (°F)	98.6–100.6
Pulse (beats per min)	60–100
Respirations (per min)	12–20
Blood Pressure (mm Hg)	
Systolic	<120
Diastolic	<80

Children, 0–1 year

Vital Sign	Range
Temperature	
Oral (°F)	96.0–99.5
Rectal (°F)	99.0–100.0
Pulse (beats per min)	80–160
Respirations (per min)	26–40
Blood Pressure (mm Hg)	
Systolic	74–100
Diastolic	50–70

Children, 1–6 years

Vital Sign	Range
Temperature	
Oral (°F)	98.5–99.5
Rectal (°F)	99.0–100.0
Pulse (beats per min)	75–130
Respirations (per min)	20–30
Blood Pressure (mm Hg)	
Systolic	80–112
Diastolic	50–80

Children, 6–11 years

Vital Sign	Range
Temperature	
Oral (°F)	97.5–99.6
Rectal (°F)	98.5–99.6
Pulse (beats per min)	70–115
Respirations (per min)	18–24
Blood Pressure (mm Hg)	
Systolic	80–120
Diastolic	50–80

Children, 11–16 years

Vital Sign	Range
Temperature	
Oral (°F)	97.6–99.6
Rectal (°F)	98.6–100.6
Pulse (beats per min)	55–110
Respirations (per min)	16–24
Blood Pressure (mm Hg)	
Systolic	88–120
Diastolic	58–80

Pulse

Characteristics

- **Rhythm**—may be regular or irregular
- **Volume**—may be weak, strong, or bounding

Locations

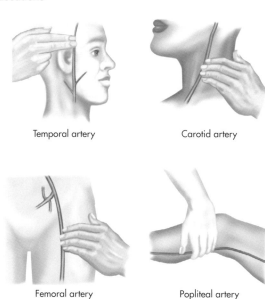

Temporal artery

Carotid artery

Femoral artery

Popliteal artery

Brachial artery

Radial artery

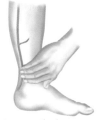

Posterior tibial artery

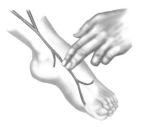

Dorsalis pedis artery

Pulse and respiration

Critical Procedure Steps

1. Gather the equipment and wash your hands.
2. Identify the patient.
3. Explain the procedure but do not say you are counting respirations.
4. Place the patient in a comfortable position with her arm resting on the table, palm down.

continued

241

5. Position yourself so you can observe or feel the chest wall movements.

6. Locate the radial pulse and place two fingers on it.

7. Count the pulse for 15 to 30 seconds if regular and 1 full minute if irregular.

8. Without letting go of the wrist, count the respirations for 1 full minute.

9. Record the pulse and respirations.

10. Document results with the date and time.

11. Report any numbers that are a significant change or outside the range.

3

General

Anatomy and Physiology

Anatomic Position

- The body is standing upright and facing forward with the arms at the sides and the palms of the hands facing forward.
- This position is used as a reference point when describing directional terms.

Body Cavities

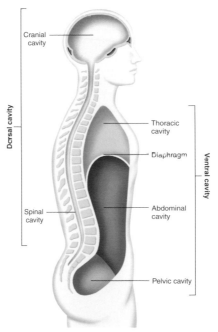

243

Body Movements

Flexion—bending a body part or decreasing the angle of a joint

Extension—straightening a body part or increasing the angle of a joint

Hyperextension—extending a body part past the normal anatomical position

Dorsiflexion—pointing the toes up

Plantarflexion—pointing the toes down

Abduction—moving a body part away from the midline of the body

Adduction—moving a body part toward the midline of the body

Rotation—twisting a body part; for example, turning your head from side to side

Circumduction—moving a body part in a circle; for example, moving your arm in a circular motion

Pronation—turning the palm of the hand down or lying face down

Supination—turning the palm of the hand up or lying face up

Inversion—turning the sole of the foot medially

Eversion—turning the sole of the foot laterally

Protraction—moving a body part anteriorly

Retraction—moving a body part posteriorly

Depression—lowering a body part; for example, lowering your shoulders

Elevation—lifting a body part; for example, elevating your shoulders as in a shrugging expression

Body Planes

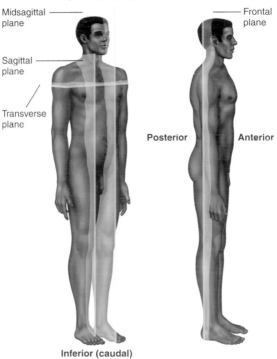

Superior (cranial)

Midsagittal plane

Sagittal plane

Transverse plane

Frontal plane

Posterior   Anterior

Inferior (caudal)

Body Quadrants and Regions

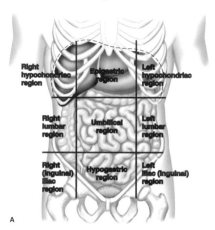

A

Right hypochondriac region

Epigastric region

Left hypochondriac region

Right lumbar region

Umbilical region

Left lumbar region

Right (inguinal) iliac region

Hypogastric region

Left iliac (inguinal) region

B

Right upper quadrant (RUQ)

Left upper quadrant (LUQ)

Right lower quadrant (RLQ)

Left lower quadrant (LLQ)

Directional Terms

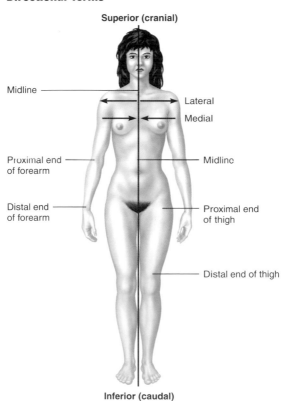

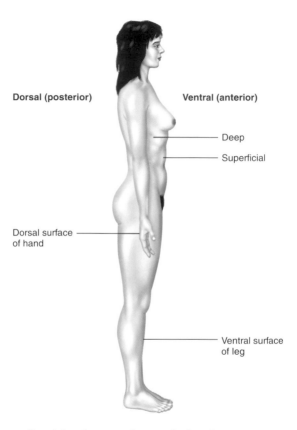

Dorsal (posterior)

Ventral (anterior)

Deep

Superficial

Dorsal surface
of hand

Ventral surface
of leg

Cranial—above or close to the head

Caudal—below or close to the feet

Ventral—toward the front of the body

Dorsal—toward the back of the body

Medial—close to the midline of the body

Lateral—farther away from the midline of the body

Proximal—close to a point of attachment or to the trunk of the body

Distal—farther away from a point of attachment or from the trunk of the body

Superficial—close to the surface of the body

Deep—more internal

Organization of the Body

Atoms—the simplest units of all matter

Matter—anything that takes up weight; includes liquids, solids, and gases

Molecule—the smallest unit into which an element can be divided and still retain its properties; it is formed when atoms bond together

Organelle—a structure within a cell that performs a specific function

Cell—the smallest living units of structure and function

Tissue—a structure that is formed when cells of the same type organize together

Organ—a structure formed by the organization of two or more different tissue types that carries out specific functions

Organ System—a system that consists of organs that join together to carry out vital functions.

Organism—a whole living being that is formed from organ systems

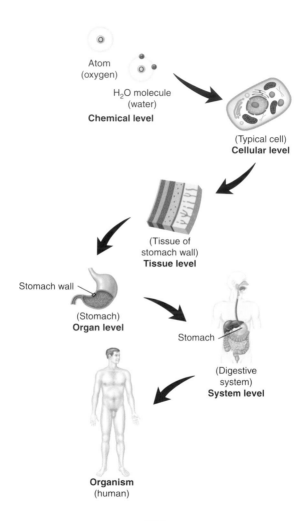

Atom
(oxygen)

H_2O molecule
(water)

Chemical level

(Typical cell)
Cellular level

(Tissue of
stomach wall)
Tissue level

Stomach wall

(Stomach)
Organ level

Stomach

(Digestive
system)
System level

Organism
(human)

Organ Systems

The integumentary system

- Functions—protection, body temperature regulation, vitamin D production, sensation, and excretion
- Organs—skin, hair, sebaceous glands, nails, and sudoriferous glands

The skeletal system

- Functions—shape, support, protection, movement, and blood cell production
- Organs—bones

The muscular system

- Functions—movement, stability, control of body openings, and heat production
- Organs—muscles, tendons, and ligaments

The cardiovascular system

- Functions—blood transport
- Organs—heart, blood, veins, and arteries

The respiratory system

- Functions—oxygen and carbon dioxide exchange
- Organs—nose, pharynx, larynx, trachea, bronchial tree, and lungs

The nervous system

- Functions—detecting and interpreting sensory information, making decisions about that information, and responding to and carrying out motor functions based on those decisions

- Organs—brain, spinal cord, and nerves

The urinary system

- Functions—removing waste products from the blood, urine elimination, regulation of blood cell production, and blood pressure regulation
- Organs—kidneys, ureters, bladder, urethra

The reproductive systems

- Functions—offspring production
- Organs
  - Male—testes, penis, prostate gland, and bulbourethral glands
  - Female—ovaries, fallopian tubes, uterus, vagina, breasts

The lymphatic and immune systems

- Functions—protect the body against infections, toxins, and cancer
- Organs—spleen, thymus, lymph nodes, lymph vessels, and lymph

The digestive system

- Functions—digestion and absorption of nutrients and waste elimination
- Organs—mouth, teeth, salivary glands, pharynx, esophagus, stomach, small intestine, large intestine, pancreas, liver, and gallbladder

The endocrine system

- Functions—regulation of all cellular chemical reactions
- Organs—hypothalamus, pituitary, pineal body, thyroid, parathyroid, thymus, adrenals, and pancreas

Communication

5 Cs of Communication

- **Completeness**—The message must contain all necessary information.
- **Clarity**—The message must be legible and free from ambiguity.
- **Conciseness**—The message must be brief and direct.
- **Courtesy**—The message must be respectful and considerate of others.
- **Cohesiveness**—The message must be organized and logical.

Telephone Screening and Procedures

Calls requiring the doctor's attention

- Emergency calls
- Calls from other doctors
- Patient requests to discuss test results, particularly abnormal results
- Reports from patients concerning unsatisfactory progress
- Requests for prescription renewals (unless previously authorized on the patient's chart)
- Personal calls

Collecting patient data

Effective methods of collecting patient data include:

- Asking open-ended questions
- Asking hypothetical questions
- Mirroring a patient's responses and verbalizing the implied
- Focusing on the patient
- Encouraging the patient to take the lead
- Encouraging the patient to provide additional information
- Encouraging the patient to evaluate his situation

Documenting a phone call

Each call should have the following information documented:

- Date and time of the call
- Name of the person for whom you took the message
- Caller's name
- Caller's telephone number (including area code and extension, if any)
- A description or an action to be taken, including comments such as "Urgent," "Please call back," "Wants to see you," "Will call back," or "Returned your call"
- The complete message
- Name or initials of the person taking the call

Handling incoming calls

- Answer the telephone promptly by the second or third ring. Hold the telephone to your ear or use a headset to hold the ear piece securely against your ear. Do not cradle the telephone with your shoulder; doing so can cause muscle strain.

- Hold the mouthpiece about an inch away from your mouth and leave one hand free to write with.
- Greet the caller first with the name of the medical office and then with your name.
- Identify the caller. Demonstrate your willingness to assist the caller by asking, "How may I help you?"
- Be courteous, calm, and pleasant no matter how hurried you are.
- Identify the nature of the call and devote your full attention to the caller.
- At the end of the call, say goodbye and use the caller's name.

Handling outgoing calls

- Plan before you call. Have all the information you need in front of you before you dial the telephone number. Plan what you will say and decide what questions to ask so that you will not have to call back for additional information.
- Double-check the telephone number. Before placing a call, always confirm the number. If in doubt, look it up in the telephone directory. If you do dial a wrong number, be sure to apologize for the mistake.
- Allow enough time, at least a minute or about eight rings, for someone to answer the telephone. When calling patients who are elderly or physically disabled, allow additional time.

- Identify yourself. After reaching the person to whom you placed the call, give your name and state that you are calling on behalf of the doctor.

- Ask if you have called at a convenient time and whether the person has time to talk with you. If it is not a good time, ask when you should call back.

- Be ready to speak as soon as the person you called answers the telephone. Do not waste the person's time while you collect your thoughts.

- If you are calling to give information, ask if the person has a pencil and piece of paper available. Do not begin with dates, times, or instructions until the person is ready to write down the information.

Telephone Etiquette

Checking for understanding

- If a call is long or complicated, summarize what was said to be sure that both you and the caller understand the information.

- Ask if the caller has any questions about what you have discussed.

Communicating feelings

- When dealing with a caller who is nervous, upset, or angry, try to show empathy.

- Communicating with empathy helps the caller feel more positive about the conversation and the medical office.

Enunciation

- Speaking clearly and distinctly
- Do not chew gum or eat while on the phone.
- Do not prop the phone between your ear and shoulder.

Exhibiting courtesy

- Project an attitude of helpfulness.
- Always use the person's name during the conversation.
- Apologize for any errors or delays.
- When ending the conversation, be sure to thank the caller before hanging up.

Giving undivided attention

- Do not try to answer the telephone while continuing to carry out another task.
- Give the caller the same undivided attention you would if the person were in the office.
- Listen carefully to get the correct information.

Handling difficult situations

- If an emergency arises while you are on the phone, ask if you can call back.
- Explain that you are currently handling an urgent matter.
- Offer to return the call in a few minutes.

Making a good impression

- How you handle telephone calls will have an impact on the public image of the medical practice.

Putting a call on hold

- Before putting a call on hold, always let the caller state the reason for the call.
- State why you need to place the call on hold.
- Explain how long you expect the wait to be.
- Ask the caller if this wait is acceptable.
- If you need to answer a second call, get the second caller's name and telephone number, and put that call on hold until you have completed the first call.

Pronunciation

- Saying the words correctly
- You may have to ask a patient to pronounce his or her name.

Remembering patients' names

- When patients are recognized by name, they are more likely to have positive feelings about the practice.
- Using a caller's name during a conversation makes the caller feel important.

Tone

- Speak with a positive and respectful tone.

Your telephone voice

- Speak directly into the receiver, otherwise your voice will be difficult to understand.
- Smile. The smile in your voice will convey your friendliness and willingness to help.
- Visualize the caller, and speak directly to that person.

- Convey a friendly and respectful interest in the caller.
- You should sound helpful and alert.
- Use language that is nontechnical and easy to understand. Never use slang.
- Speak at a natural pace, not too quickly or too slowly.
- Use a normal conversational tone.
- Try to vary your pitch while you are talking.
- Make the caller feel important.

Ending the conversation
- Take a few seconds to complete the call so that the caller feels properly cared for and satisfied.
- Complete the call by summarizing the important points of the conversation and thanking the caller.
- Let the caller hang up first.

Telephone Triage
Definition: A process of deciding what necessary action to take

Tips for Taking Messages
- Always have a pen or pencil and paper on hand.
- Jot down notes as the information is given.
- Verify information, especially the spelling of patient or caller names and the correct spelling of medications.

- Verify the correct callback number.
- When taking a phone message for the physician, never make a commitment on behalf of the physician by saying, "I'll have the physician call you." An appropriate response would be, "I will give your message to the physician."

Legal and Ethical Issues, Including HIPAA

4 Cs of Medical Malpractice Prevention

1. Caring—Showing patients that you care about them may result in an improvement in their medical condition and, if you are sincere, decreases the likelihood that patients will feel the need to sue if treatment has unsatisfactory results or adverse events occur.

2. Communication—If you communicate in a professional manner and clearly ask for confirmation that you have been understood, you will earn respect and trust with your patients and other members of the allied health team.

3. Competence—Be competent in your skills and job knowledge and maintain and update your knowledge and skills frequently through continuing education.

4. Charting—Documentation is proof of competence. Make sure that all current reports and consultations have been reviewed by the physician and evident in the chart. Chart every conversation or interaction you have with a patient.

Credit and Collection Laws

Law	Requirements
Equal Credit Opportunity Act (ECOA)	• Creditors may not discriminate against applicants on the basis of sex, marital status, race, national origin, religion, or age • Creditors may not discriminate because an applicant receives public assistance income or has exercised rights under the Consumer Credit Protection Act
Fair Credit Reporting Act (FCRA)	This act requires credit bureaus to supply correct and complete information to businesses to use in evaluating a person's application for credit, insurance, or a job
Fair Debt Collection Practices Act (FDCPA)	This act requires debt collectors to treat debtors fairly. It prohibits certain collection tactics, such as harassment, false statements, threats, and unfair practices.
Truth in Lending Act (TLA)	This act requires creditors to provide applicants with accurate and complete credit costs and terms.

HIPAA and Patient Rights

- Patients have the right to choose a physician.
- Patients also have the right to terminate a physician's services.

HIPAA Definitions

Use

Performing any of the following actions to individually identifiable health information by employees or other members of an organization's workforce:

- Sharing
- Employing
- Applying
- Utilizing
- Examining
- Analyzing

Disclosure

Performing any of the following actions so that the information is outside the entity:

- Releasing
- Transferring
- Providing access to
- Divulging in any manner

Information is disclosed when it is transmitted between or among organizations.

HIPAA "Do's and Don'ts"—When and What to Disclose

YOU SHOULD KNOW

1. When in doubt about whether to release information, it is better not to release it.

2. It is the patient's, not the doctor's, right to keep patient information confidential. If the patient wants to disclose the information, it is unethical for the physician not to do so.

3. All patients should be treated with the same degree of confidentiality, whatever the health-care professional's personal opinion of the patient might be.

4. You should be aware of all applicable laws and of the regulations of agencies such as public health departments.

5. When it is necessary to break confidentiality and when there is a conflict between ethics and confidentiality, discuss it with the patient. If the law does not dictate what to do in the situation, the attending physician should make the judgment based on the urgency of the situation and any danger that might be posed to the patient or others.

6. Get written approval from the patient before releasing information. For common situations, the patient should sign a standard release-of-records form.

HIPAA Security Rule

- A security officer must be assigned the responsibility for the medical facility's security.
- All staff, including management, receives security awareness training.

- Medical facilities must implement audit controls to record and examine staff who have logged into information systems that contain PHI.
- Organizations limit physical access to medical facilities that contain electronic PHI.
- Organizations must conduct risk analyses to determine information security risks and vulnerabilities.
- Organizations must establish policies and procedures that allow access to electronic PHI on a need-to-know basis.

HIPAA Privacy Rule

- The core of the Privacy Rule is the protection, use, and disclosure of protected health information (PHI). This rule protects individuals' medical records and other personal health information.

PHI

- Name
- Address
- Phone numbers
- Fax number
- Dates (birth, death, admission, discharge, etc.)
- Social Security number
- E-mail address
- Medical record numbers
- Health plan beneficiary numbers
- Account numbers
- Certificate or license numbers

- Vehicle identifiers and serial numbers, including license plate numbers
- Device identifiers and serial numbers
- Web Universal Resource Locators (URLs)
- Internet Protocol (IP) address numbers

Chart security

- Charts that contain a patient's name or other identifiers cannot be in view at the front reception area or nurse's station. Some offices have placed charts in plain jackets to prevent information from being seen.
- Charts must be stored out of the view of a public area, so that they cannot be seen by unauthorized individuals.
- Charts should be placed on the filing shelves without the patient name showing.
- Charts should be locked when not in use. Many facilities have purchased filing equipment that can be locked and unlocked without limiting the availability of patient information.
- Every staff member who uses patient information must be logged and a confidentiality statement signed. Signatures of staff should be on file with the office.

Clinical area and computer security

- Log off or turn your monitor off when leaving your terminal or computer.
- When placing charts in exam room racks or in shelves, the name of the patient or other identifiers must be concealed from other patients.

- HIPAA does not have a regulation about calling patients' names in the reception area, but to increase privacy in your facility, you may suggest a numbering system to identify patients.
- When discussing a patient with another staff member or with the physician, make sure your voice is lowered and that all doors to the exam rooms are closed. Avoid discussing patient conditions in heavy traffic areas.
- When discussing a condition with a patient, make sure that you are in a private room or area where no one can hear you.
- Avoid discussing patients in lunchrooms, hallways, or any place in a medical facility where someone can overhear you.

Copier security

- Do not leave confidential documents anywhere on the copier where others can read the information.
- Do not discard copies in a shared trash container, shred them.
- If a paper jam occurs, be sure to remove from the copier the copy or partial copy that caused the jam.

Fax security

- **Fax cover page**—State clearly on the fax cover sheet that confidential and protected health information is included. Further state that the information included is to be protected and must not be shared or disclosed without the appropriate authorizations from the patient.

- **Location of the fax machine**—Keep the fax machine in an area that is not accessible by individuals who are not authorized to view PHI.

- **Faxes with protected health information**—Faxes that your office receives with PHI must be stored promptly in a protected, secure area.

- **Fax number**—Always confirm the accuracy of fax numbers to minimize the possibility of faxes being sent to the wrong person. Call people to tell them the fax is being sent.

- **Confirmation**—Program the fax machine to print a confirmation for all faxes sent, and staple the confirmation sheet to each document sent.

- **Training**—Train all staff members to understand the importance of safeguarding PHI sent or received via fax.

Printer security

- Do not print confidential material on a printer shared by other departments or in an area when others can read the material.

- Do not leave printer unattended while printing confidential material.

- Before leaving the printing area, check to be sure all computer disks containing confidential information and all printed material have been collected.

- Be certain that the print job is sent to the right printer location.

- Do not discard printouts in a shared trash container; shred them.

Reception area security

- Log off or turn your monitor off when leaving your terminal or computer.

- The computer must be placed in an area where other patients cannot see the screen.

- Many facilities are purchasing flat screen monitors to prevent visibility to the screen.

- The sign-in sheet must be monitored and not left out in patient view. The names of patients must be blacked out so the next patient cannot read the names. It is best to put another system in place and to eliminate the sign-in sheet.

- Many offices are reviewing the reception area with regard to phone conversations. Some offices are creating call centers away from the reception/waiting area.

Appendixes

Appendix I
Ergonomics

Critical Procedure Steps

A. Patient Transfer from a Wheelchair

Never risk injuring yourself; call for assistance when in doubt. As a rule you should not attempt to lift more than 35% of your body weight.

Preparation Before Transfer

1. Identify the patient and introduce yourself.

2. Wash your hands.

3. Explain the procedure in detail.

4. Position the wheelchair at a right angle to the end of the examining table. This position reduces the distance between the wheelchair and the end of the examining table across which the patient must move.

5. Lock the wheels of the wheelchair to prevent the wheelchair from moving during the transfer.

6. Lift the patient's feet and fold back the foot and leg supports of the wheelchair.

7. Place the patient's feet on the floor, and ensure that the patient will not slip on the floor. (The patient should have shoes or slippers with

continued

nonskid soles.) Place your feet in front of the patient's feet to prevent further slipping.

8. If needed, place a step stool in front of the table, and place the patient's feet flat on the stool.

Transferring the Patient by Yourself

9. Face the patient, spread your feet apart, align your knees with the patient's knees, and bend your knees slightly. (If you lift while bending at the waist instead of bending your knees, you can cause serious injury to your back.)

10. Have the patient hold on to your shoulders.

11. Place your arms around the patient, under the patient's arms.

12. Tell the patient that you will lift on the count of three, and ask the patient to support as much of his own weight as possible (if he is able).

13. At the count of three, lift the patient.

14. Pivot the patient to bring the back of the patient's knees against the table.

15. Gently lower the patient into a sitting position on the table. If the patient cannot sit unassisted, help him move into a supine position.

16. Move the wheelchair out of the way.

17. Assist the patient with disrobing as necessary, providing a gown and drape.

Transferring the Patient With Assistance

9. Working with your partner, both of you face the patient, spread your feet apart, position

yourselves so that one of each of your knees is aligned with the patient's knees, and bend your knees slightly. (If you lift while bending at your waist instead of bending your knees, you can cause serious injury to your back.)

10. Have the patient place one hand on each of your shoulders and hold on.

11. Each of you places your outermost arm around the patient, one under each of the patient's arms. Then interlock your wrists.

12. Tell the patient that you will lift on the count of three, and ask the patient to support as much of his own weight as possible (if he is able).

13. At the count of three, you should lift the patient together.

14. The stronger of the two of you should pivot the patient to bring the back of the patient's knees against the table.

15. Working together, gently lower the patient into a sitting position on the table. If the patient cannot sit unassisted, help him move into a supine position.

16. Move the wheelchair out of the way.

17. Assist the patient with disrobing as necessary, providing a gown and drape.

B. Computer Ergonomics

If you use a keyboard for extended periods, you should practice proper techniques to prevent carpal tunnel syndrome.

continued

- While seated, hold your arms relaxed at your sides, and check to make sure that your keyboard is positioned slightly higher than your elbows. As you input, keep your elbows at your sides and relax your shoulders.

- Use only your fingers to press keys, and do not use more pressure than necessary. Use a wrist rest, and keep your wrists relaxed and straight.

- When you need to strike difficult-to-reach keys, move your whole hand rather than stretching your fingers. When you need to press two keys at the same time, such as "Control" and "F1," use two hands.

- Try to break up long periods of keyboard work with other tasks that do not require computer use.

Tips for Relieving Symptoms
If you have symptoms of carpal tunnel syndrome, try these suggestions for relief.

- Elevate your arms.
- Wear a splint on the hand and forearm.
- Discuss your symptoms with a physician, who may prescribe medication.

Appendix II
Abbreviations

a before

a.c. before meals

ADD attention deficit disorder

ADL activities of daily living

ad lib as desired

ADT admission, discharge, transfer

AIDS acquired immunodeficiency syndrome

a.m.a. against medical advice

AMA American Medical Association

amp. ampule

amt amount

aq., AQ water; aqueous

ausc. auscultation

ax axis

Bib, bib drink

b.i.d., bid, BID twice a day

BM bowel movement

BP, B/P blood pressure

BPC blood pressure check

BPH benign prostatic hypertrophy

BSA body surface area

$\overline{c}.,\overline{c}$ with

Ca calcium; cancer

cap, caps capsules

CBC complete blood (cell) count

C.C., CC chief complaint

CDC Centers for Disease Control and Prevention

CHF congestive heart failure

chr chronic

CNS central nervous system

Comp, comp compound

COPD chronic obstructive pulmonary disease

CP chest pain

CPE complete physical exam

CPR cardiopulmonary resuscitation

CSF cerebrospinal fluid

CT computed tomography

CV cardiovascular

d day

D&C dilation and curettage

DEA Drug Enforcement Administration

Dil, dil dilute

DM diabetes mellitus

DOB date of birth

DTP diphtheria-tetanus-pertussis vaccine

Dr. doctor

DTs delirium tremens

D/W dextrose in water

Dx, dx diagnosis

ECG, EKG electrocardiogram

ED emergency department

EEG electroencephalogram

EENT eyes, ears, nose, and throat

EP established patient

ER emergency room

ESR erythrocyte sedimentation rate

FBS fasting blood sugar

FDA Food and Drug Administration

FH family history

Fl, fl, fld fluid

F/u follow-up

Fx fracture

GBS gallbladder series

GI gastrointestinal

Gm gram

gr grain

gt, gtt drops

GTT glucose tolerance test

GU genitourinary

GYN gynecology

HB, Hgb hemoglobin

HEENT head, ears, eyes, nose, throat

HIV human immunodeficiency virus

HO history of

h.s., hs, HS hour of sleep/at bedtime

Hx history

ICU intensive care unit

I&D incision and drainage

I&O intake and output

IM intramuscular

inf. infusion; inferior

inj injection

IT inhalation therapy

IUD intrauterine device

IV intravenous

KUB kidneys, ureters, bladder

L1, L2, etc. lumbar vertebrae

lab laboratory

liq liquid

LLL left lower lobe

LLQ left lower quadrant

LMP last menstrual period

LUQ left upper quadrant

MI myocardial infarction

mL milliliter

MM mucous membrane

MRI magnetic resonance imaging

MS multiple sclerosis

NB newborn

NED no evidence of disease

no. number

noc, noct night

npo, NPO nothing by mouth

NPT new patient

NS normal saline

NSAID nonsteroidal anti-inflammatory drug

NTP normal temperature and pressure

N&V nausea and vomiting

NYD not yet diagnosed

OB obstetrics

OC oral contraceptive

OD overdose

O.D., OD right eye

oint ointment

OOB out of bed

OPD outpatient department

OPS outpatient services

OR operating room

O.S., OS left eye

OTC over-the-counter

O.U., OU both eyes

P&P Pap smear (Papanicolaou smear) and pelvic exam

PA posteroanterior

Pap Pap smear

Path pathology

p.c., pc after meals

PE physical exam

per by, with

PH past history

PID pelvic inflammatory disease

p/o postoperative

POMR problem-oriented medical record

PMFSH past medical, family, social history

PMS premenstrual syndrome

p.r.n., prn, PRN whenever necessary

Pt patient

PT physical therapy

PTA prior to admission

PVC premature ventricular contraction

pulv powder

q. every

q2, q2h every 2 hours

q.a.m., qam every morning

q.h., qh every hour

qhs every night, at bedtime

q.i.d., QID four times a day

qns, QNS quantity not sufficient

qs, QS quantity sufficient

RA rheumatoid arthritis; right atrium

RBC red blood cells; red blood (cell) count

RDA recommended dietary allowance,
recommended daily allowance

REM rapid eye movement

RF rheumatoid factor

RLL right lower lobe

RLQ right lower quadrant

R/O rule out

ROM range of motion

ROS/SR review of systems/systems review

RUQ right upper quadrant

RV right ventricle

Rx prescription, take

SAD seasonal affective disorder

subq, SubQ subcutaneously

SIDS sudden infant death syndrome

Sig directions

sig sigmoidoscopy

SOAP subjective, objective, assessment, plan

SOB shortness of breath

sol solution

S/R suture removal

$\overline{\text{ss}}$ one-half

Staph staphylococcus

stat, STAT immediately

STD sexually transmitted disease

Strep streptococcus

subling, SL sublingual

surg surgery

S/W saline in water

SX symptoms

T1, T2, etc. thoracic vertebrae

T & A tonsillectomy and adenoidectomy

tab tablet

TB tuberculosis

TBS, tbs. tablespoon

TIA transient ischemic attack

t.i.d., tid, TID three times a day

tinc, tinct, tr tincture

TMJ temporomandibular joint

top topically

TPR temperature, pulse, and respiration

tsp teaspoon

TSH thyroid stimulating hormone

Tx treatment

UA urinalysis

UCHD usual childhood diseases

UGI upper gastrointestinal

ung, ungt ointment

URI upper respiratory infection

US ultrasound

UTI urinary tract infection

VA visual acuity

VD venereal disease

Vf visual field

VS vital signs

WBC white blood cells; white blood (cell) count

WNL within normal limits

wt weight

y/o year old

Appendix III
Commonly Misspelled Terms

A. Medical Terms

anergic	anesthetic
aneurysm	anteflexion
arrhythmia	asepsis
asthma	auricle
benign	bilirubin
bronchial	calcaneus
capillary	cervical
chancre	choroid
chromosome	cirrhosis
clavicle	curettage
cyanosis	defibrillator
desiccation	diluent
dissect	eosinophil
epididymis	epistaxis
erythema	eustachian
fissure	flexure
fomites	glaucoma

glomerular	gonorrhea
hemocytometer	hemorrhage
hemorrhoids	homeostasis
humerus	ileum
ilium	infarction
inoculate	intussusception
ischemia	ischium
larynx	leukemia
leukocyte	malaise
menstruation	metastasis
muscle	neuron
nosocomial	occlusion
ophthalmology	oscilloscope
osseous	palliative
parasite	parenteral
parietal	paroxysm
pericardium	perineum
peristalsis	peritoneum
pharynx	pituitary
plantar	pleurisy
pneumonia	polyp
prescription	prophylaxis
prostate	prosthesis
pruritus	psoriasis

psychiatrist	pyrexia
respiration	rheumatism
roentgenology	scirrhous
serous	specimen
sphincter	sphygmomanometer
squamous	staphylococcus
surgeon	vaccine
vein	venous
wheal	

B. Other Terms

absence	accept
accessible	accommodate
accumulate	achieve
acquire	adequate
advantageous	affect
aggravate	all right
a lot	already
altogether	analysis
analyze	apparatus
apparent	appearance
appropriate	approximate
argument	assistance
associate	auxiliary

balloon	bankruptcy
believe	benefited
brochure	bulletin
business	category
changeable	characteristic
cigarette	circumstance
clientele	committee
comparative	complement
compliment	concede
conscientious	conscious
controversy	corroborate
counsel	courtesy
defendant	definite
dependent	description
desirable	development
dilemma	disappear
disappoint	disapprove
disastrous	discreet
discrete	discrimination
dissatisfied	dissipate
earnest	ecstasy
effect	eligible
embarrass	emphasis
entrepreneur	envelope

environment	exceed
except	exercise
exhibit	exhilaration
existence	fantasy
fascinate	February
fluorescent	forty
grammar	grievance
guarantee	handkerchief
height	humorous
hygiene	incidentally
indispensable	inimitable
insistent	irrelevant
irresistible	irritable
its	it's
labeled	laboratory
led	leisure
liable	liaison
license	liquefy
maintenance	maneuver
miscellaneous	misspelled
necessary	noticeable
occasion	occurrence
offense	oscillate
paid	pamphlet

panicky	paradigm
parallel	paralyze
pastime	persevere
persistent	personal
personnel	persuade
phenomenon	plagiarism
pleasant	possession
precede	precedent
predictable	predominant
prejudice	preparation
prerogative	prevalent
principal	principle
privilege	procedure
proceed	professor
pronunciation	psychiatry
psychology	pursue
questionnaire	rearrange
recede	receive
recommend	referral
relieve	repetition
rescind	resume
rhythm	ridiculous
schedule	secretary
seize	separate

similar	sizable
stationary	stationery
stomach	subpoena
succeed	suddenness
supersede	surprise
tariff	technique
temperament	temperature
thorough	transferred
truly	tyrannize
unnecessary	until
vacillate	vacuum
vegetable	vicious
warrant	Wednesday
weird	

Appendix IV
Medical Notation Symbols

Apothecaries' Weights and Measures

ℨ	dram
℥	ounce
fℨ	fluidounce
O	pint
lb	pound

Other Weights and Measures

#	pounds
°	degrees
′	foot; minute
″	inch; second
μm	micrometer
μ	micron (former term for micrometer)
mμ	millimicron; nanometer
mEq	milliequivalent
mL	milliliter
dL	deciliter
mg%	milligrams percent; milligrams per 100 mL

Abbreviations

$\overline{aa}$, $\overline{AA}$	of each
$\overline{c}$	with
M	mix (Latin *misce*)
m-	meta-
o-	ortho-
p-	para-
$\overline{p}$	after
$\overline{s}$	without
ss, $\overline{ss}$	one-half (Latin *semis*)

Mathematical Functions and Terms

#	number
$+$	plus; positive; acid reaction
$-$	minus; negative; alkaline reaction
$\pm$	plus or minus; either positive or negative; indefinite
$\times$	multiply; magnification; crossed with, hybrid
$\div$, /	divided by
$=$	equal to
$\approx$	approximately equal to
$>$	greater than; from which is derived
$<$	less than; derived from
$\not<$	not less than
$\not>$	not greater than
$\leq$	equal to or less than

$\geq$	equal to or greater than
$\neq$	not equal to
$\sqrt{}$	square root
$\sqrt[3]{}$	cube root
∞	infinity
:	ratio; "is to"
$\therefore$	therefore
%	percent
π	pi (3.14159)—the ratio of circumference of a circle to its diameter

Chemical Notations

Δ	change; heat
$\rightleftharpoons$	reversible reaction
$\uparrow$	increase
$\downarrow$	decrease

Warnings

$\mathbb{C}$	Schedule I controlled substance
$\mathbb{C}$	Schedule II controlled substance
$\mathbb{C}$	Schedule III controlled substance
$\mathbb{C}$	Schedule IV controlled substance
$\mathbb{C}$	Schedule V controlled substance
☠	poison
☢	radiation
☣	biohazard

Others

Rx	prescription; take
□, ♂	male
○, ♀	female
†	one
††	two
†††	three

Appendix V
Medical Prefixes

Prefix	Meaning
a-, an-	without, not
ab-	from, away
ad-	to, toward
adeno-	gland, glandular
aero-	air
ambi-, amph-, amphi-	both, on both sides, around
andr-, andro-	man, male
angio-	blood vessel
ano-	anus
ante-	before
antero-	in front of
anti-	against, opposing
arterio-	artery
arthro-	joint
auto-	self

continued

Prefix	Meaning
bi-	twice, double
bili-	bile
bio-	life
blasto-, blast-	developing stage
brachy-	short
brady-	slow
broncho-	bronchial
cardio-	heart
cata-	down, lower, under
centi-	hundred
cephal-, cephalo-	head
cerebr-, cerebro-	brain
chol-, chole-, cholo-	gall
chondro-	cartilage
chromo-	color
circum-	around
co-, com-, con-	together, with
colo-	colon
colp-, colpo-	vagina

Prefix	Meaning
contra-	against
cost-, costo-	rib
crani-, cranio-	skull
cryo-	cold
cysto-	bladder
cyto-	cell, cellular
dacry-, dacryo-	tears, lacrimal apparatus
dactyl-, dactylo-	finger, toe
de-	down, from
deca-	ten
deci-	tenth
demi-	half
dent-, denti-, dento-	teeth
derma-, dermat-, dermato-, derm-	skin
dextro-	to the right
di-	double, twice
dia-	through, apart, between
dipla-, diplo-	double, twin

continued

Prefix	Meaning
dis-	apart, away from
dorsi-, dorso-	back
dynia-	pain
dys-	difficult, painful, bad, abnormal
e-, ec-, ecto-	away, from, without, outside
em-, en-	in, into, inside
encephalo-	brain
endo-	within, inside
entero-	intestine
ento-	within, inner
epi-	on, above
erythro-	red
esthesio-,	sensation
eu-	good
ex-, exo-	outside of, beyond, without
extra-	outside of, beyond, in addition
fibro-	connective tissue
fore-	before, in front of

Prefix	Meaning
galact-, galacto-	milk
astr-, gastro-	stomach
glosso-	tongue
gluco-, glycol-	sugar, sweet
gyn-, gyno-, gyne-, gyneco-	woman, female
haemo-, hemato-, hem-, hemo-	blood
hemi-	half
hepa-, hepar-, hepato-	liver
herni-	rupture
hetero-	other, unlike
histo-	tissue
homeo-, homo-	same, like
hydra-, hydro-	water
hyper-	above, over, increased, excessive
hypo-	below, under, decreased
hyster-, hystero-	uterus
ictero-	jaundice
idio-	personal, self-produced

continued

Prefix	Meaning
ileo-	ileum
im-, in-, ir-	not
in-	in, into
infra-	beneath
inter-	between, among
intra-, intro-	into, within, during
juxta-	near, nearby
karyo-	nucleus, nut
kata-, kath-	down, lower, under
kera-, kerato-	horn, hardness, cornea
kineto-,	motion
lact-	milk
laparo-	abdomen
latero-	side
leuco-, leuko-	white
levo-	to the left
lipo-	fat
lith-	stone
macro-	large, long

Prefix	Meaning
mal-	bad
mast-, masto-	breast
med-, medi-	middle
mega-, megalo-,	large, great
meio-	contraction
melan-, melano-	black
meno-	month
mes-, meso-	middle
meta-	beyond
metro-, metra-	uterus
micro-	small
mio-	smaller, less
mono-	single, one
multi-	many
my-, myo-	muscle
myel-, myelo-	marrow
narco-	sleep
nas-, naso-	nose
necro-	dead

continued

Prefix	Meaning
neo-	new
nephr-, nephro-	kidney
neuro-	nerve
niter-, nitro-	nitrogen
non-, not-	no
nucleo-	nucleus
ob-	against
oculo-	eye
odont-	tooth
olig-, oligo-	few, less than normal
onco-	tumor
oo-	ovum, egg
oophor-	ovary
ophthalmo-	eye
orchid-	testicle
ortho-	straight
os-	mouth, bone
oste-, osteo-	bone
oto-	ear

Prefix	Meaning
oxy-	sharp, acid
pachy-	thick
paedo-, pedo-	child
pan-	all, every
par-, para-	alongside of, with; woman who has given birth
path-, patho-	disease, suffering
ped-, pedi-, pedo-	foot
per-	through, excessive
peri-	around
pes-	foot
phag-, phago-,	eating, consuming, swallowing
pharyngo-	throat, pharynx
phlebo-	vein
pleuro-	side, rib
pluri-	more, several
pneo-	breathing
pneumo-	air, lungs
poly-	many, much

continued

Prefix	Meaning
post-	after, behind
pre, pro-	before, in front of
presby-, presbyo-	old age
primi-	first
procto-	rectum
pseudo-	false
psych-	the mind
pulmon-, pulmono-	lung
pyelo-	pelvis (renal)
pyo-	pus
pyro-	fever, heat
quadri-	four
re-	back, again
reni-, reno-	kidney
retro-	backward, behind
rhino-	nose
sacchar-	sugar
sacro-	sacrum
salpingo-	tube, fallopian

Prefix	Meaning
sarco-	flesh
sclero-	hard, sclera
semi-	half
septi-, septic-, septico-	poison, infection
steno-	contracted, narrow
stereo-	firm, solid, three-dimensional
stomato-	mouth
sub-	under
super-, supra-,	above, upon, excess
sym-, syn-	with, together
tachy-	fast
tele-	distant, far
teno-, tenoto-	tendon
tetra-	four
thermo-	heat
thio-	sulfur
thoraco-	chest
thrombo-	blood clot
thyro-	thyroid gland

continued

Prefix	Meaning
tomo-	incision, section
trans-	across
tri-	three
tropho-	nutrition, growth
ultra-	beyond, excess
uni-	one
urino-, uro-	urine, urinary organs
utero-	uterus
vaso-	vessel
ventri-, ventro-	abdomen
xanth-	yellow

Appendix VI
Medical Suffixes

Suffix	Meaning
-ad	to, toward
-aesthesia	sensation
-al	characterized by
-algia	pain
-ase	enzyme
-asthenia	weakness
-cele	swelling, tumor
-centesis	puncture, tapping
-cidal	killing
-cide	causing death
-cise	cut
-coele	cavity
-cyst	bladder, bag
-cyte	cell, cellular
-ectomy	cutting out, surgical removal

continued

Suffix	Meaning
-emesis	vomiting
-emia	blood
-esthesia	sensation
-form	shape
-fuge	driving away
-gene, -genic, -genetic, -genous	arising from, origin, formation
-gram	recorded information
-graph	instrument for recording
-graphy	the process of recording
-gravida	pregnant female
-ia	condition
-iasis	condition of
-ic, -ical	pertaining to
-ism	condition, process, theory
-itis	inflammation of
-ium	membrane
-ize	to cause to be, to become, to treat by special method
-kinesis, -kinetic	motion

Suffix	Meaning
-lepsis, -lepsy	seizure, convulsion
-logy	science of, study of
-lysis	setting free, disintegration, decomposition
-malacia	abnormal softening
-mania	insanity, abnormal desire
-meter	measure
-metry	process of measuring
-nuli	none
-odynia	pain
-oid	resembling
-ole	small, little
-oma	tumor
-opia	vision
-opsy	to view
-osis	disease, condition of
-ostomy	to make a mouth, opening
-otomy	incision, surgical cutting
-ous	having

continued

Suffix	Meaning
-pathy	disease, suffering
-penia	too few, lack, decreased
-pexy	surgical fixation
-phage	eating, consuming, swallowing
-phobia	fear, abnormal fear
-phylaxis	protection
-plasia	formation or development
-plastic	molded
-plasty	operation to reconstruct, surgical repair
-plegia	paralysis
-pod	foot
-rrhage, -rrhagia	abnormal or excessive discharge, hemorrhage, flow
-rrhaphy	suture of
-rrhea	flow, discharge
-sclerosis	hardening
-scopy	examining
-spasm	cramp or twitching

Suffix	Meaning
-stasis	stoppage
-stomy	opening
-therapy	treatment
-thermy	heat
-tome	cutting instrument
-tomy	incision, section
-tripsy	surgical crushing
-trophy	turning, tendency
-uria	urine

Appendix VII
Common Spanish Phrases

English Term or Phrase	Spanish Translation and Pronunciation
Do you speak English?	¿Habla usted inglés? *ah-blah ooh-stead een-glase*
Do you understand English?	¿Entiende usted inglés? *in-tee-in-day ooh-stead een-glase*
I do not speak Spanish well.	Yo no hablo español bien. *yo no ah-blow ess-pan-yole bee-yen*
Please speak more slowly.	Hable más despacio por favor. *ah-blay mahss deh-spah-see-yo pore fah-vore*
Please repeat.	Repita por favor. *ray-pee-tah pore fah-vore*
I don't understand.	No entiendo. No comprendo. *no in-tee-in-doe. No kom-pren-doe*

English Term or Phrase	Spanish Translation and Pronunciation
Are you a family member?	¿Es usted miembro de la familia? *ess ooh-stead mee-em-broe day lah fah-mee-lee-yah*
Are you a friend?	¿Es usted amigo/amiga de la familia? *ess ooh-stead ah-mee-goe/ ah-mee-gah day lah fah-mee-lee-yah*
Can you interpret for me (us)?	¿Puede servir de intérprete? *pway-day sehr-veer day in-tehr-pray-tay*
Can you translate for me (us)?	¿Puede traducir? *pway-day trah-due-sehr*
Have you been ill?	¿Usted ha estado enfermo/ enferma? *ooh-stead ah ess-tah-doe in-fehr-moe/in-fehr-mah*
What is your full name?	¿Cuál es su nombre completo? *kwall ess soo nome-bray kom-plet-o*
What is your date of birth?	¿Cuál es la fecha de su nacimiento? *kwall ess lah feh-cha day soo nah-see-mee-in-toe*

continued

English Term or Phrase	Spanish Translation and Pronunciation
What is your address?	¿Cuál es su dirección? *kwall es soo dee-rek-see-own*
What is your phone number?	¿Cuál es su número de teléfono? *kwall ess soo new-mehr-oh day tell-ayh-foe-noe*
yes	sí *see*
no	no *no*
maybe	quizás/a lo major *key-zahss/ah low mah-yore*
up	arriba *ah-ree-bah*
down	abajo *ah-bah-hoe*
left	a la izquierda *a lah eez-key-air-dah*
right	a la derecha *a lah dehr-retch-ah*
in	adentro *ah-den-troh*
out	afuera *ah-fweh-rah*

English Term or Phrase	Spanish Translation and Pronunciation
around	alrededor *al-ray-day-door*
above	sobre *so-bray*
here	aquí *ah-key*
there	allá *ah-yah*
front	enfrente *en-fren-tay*
back	detrás *day-trahs*
top	arriba *ah-ree-bah*
bottom	abajo *ah-bah-hoe*
I don't know	No sé. *No say*
Numbers:	Números *New-mehr-ose*
0	cero *seh-roe*
1	uno *ooh-noe*

continued

English Term or Phrase	Spanish Translation and Pronunciation
2	dos *dose*
3	tres *trace*
4	cuatro *kwah-troe*
5	cinco *sink-o*
6	seis *saise*
7	siete *see-yet-ay*
8	ocho *owe-choe*
9	nueve *new-ev-ay*
10	diez *dee-yes*
11	once *own-say*
12	doce *doe-say*
13	trece *tray-say*

English Term or Phrase	Spanish Translation and Pronunciation
14	catorce *kah-tore-say*
15	quince *keen-say*
16	dieciséis *dee-yes-ee-saise*
17	diecisiete *dee-yes-ee-see-yetay*
18	dieciocho *dee-yes-ee-owecho*
19	diecinueve *dee-yes-ee-new-evay*
20	veinte *ben-tay*
30	treinta *tren-tah*
40	cuarenta *kwar-in-tah*
50	cincuenta *sink-went-ah*
60	sesenta *sess-in-tah*
70	setenta *set-in-tah*

continued

English Term or Phrase	Spanish Translation and Pronunciation
80	ochenta *owe-chen-tah*
90	noventa *noe-ben-tah*
100	cien *see-in*
Days of the week:	Días de la semana
Sunday	Domingo *doe-ming-oh*
Monday	Lunes *loo-nayse*
Tuesday	Martes *mar-tayse*
Wednesday	Miércoles *mee-yehr-ko-layse*
Thursday	Jueves *hway-vayse*
Friday	Viernes *vee-yehr-nayse*
Saturday	Sábado *sah-bah-doe*
yesterday	ayer *ah-yehr*

English Term or Phrase	Spanish Translation and Pronunciation
today	hoy *oy*
tomorrow	mañana *mah-nya-nah*
this morning	esta mañana *ess-tah mah-nya-na*
this afternoon	esta tarde *ess-tah tahr-day*
this evening	esta noche *ess-tah no-chay*
day	día *dee-ah*
week	semana *say-mah-nah*
month	mes *mehs*
Months of the year:	Meses del año:
January	Enero *Eh-nehr-oh*
February	Febrero *feh-brer-oh*
March	Marzo *mahr-soh*

continued

English Term or Phrase	Spanish Translation and Pronunciation
April	Abril *ah-breel*
May	Mayo *my-oh*
June	Junio *hoo-nee-oh*
July	Julio *hoo-lee-oh*
August	Agosto *ah-gohst-oh*
September	Septiembre *Sep-tee-em-bray*
October	Octubre *ohk-too-bray*
November	Noviembre *no-vee-em-bray*
December	Diciembre *dee-cee-em-bray*
year	año *ah-nyo*
What kind of pain do you have?	¿Cómo es su dolor? *ko-mo ess soo doe-lohr*
In what way are you ill today?	¿Cómo se siente hoy? *ko-mo say see-in-tay oy.*

English Term or Phrase	Spanish Translation and Pronunciation
I am checking your pulse.	Estoy tomándole el pulso. *ess-toy toe-mahn-doe-lay ell pool-so*
I am checking your blood pressure.	Estoy tomándole la presión arterial. *ess-toy toe-mahn-doe-lay lah press-ee-ohn ahr-teer-ee-ahl*
I need to listen to your heart and lungs.	Necesito escuchar su corazón y sus pulmones. *ness-ess-see-toe ess-koo-char soo kor-ah-zone ee soos pool-mone-ase*
I need to touch you now.	Necesito palparlo ahora. *ness-ess-ee-toe pal-par-loe ah-ora*
Please open your shirt.	Por favor ábrase la camisa. *pore fah-vore ah-brah-say lah kah-mee-sah*

Appendix VIII
ASL American Manual Alphabet

A
Palm is always forward except where noted

B

C
Palm forward thumb bent out

D

E
Thumb also often lower (like a claw)

F

G
Palm in

H
Palm in

I

J

K

L

M

N

O
Palm faces opposite side of body

P
Index finger points out

Q

Like p but points
down and unseen
fingers curled in

R　**S**　**T**　**U**

V　**W**　**X**　**Y**　**Z**

Palm forward; thumb
can be over fingers;
whole palm can be
slanted to side
away from body

0　**1**　**2**　**3**　**4**

5　**6**　**7**　**8**　**9**

Appendix IX
Local Emergency Numbers

Alcohol and Drug Abuse Center _____

Behavioral Health _____

Children and Family Crises Services _____

Community Health _____

Domestic Violence Hotline _____

Emergency Management and
Hazard Control _____

Local Homeless Shelters _____

Local Red Cross _____

National Suicide Prevention Hotline   800-273-TALK
(8255)

Nonemergency Police _____

Poison Control Center   800-222-1222

    Local Number _____

Sexual Assault Hotline _____

Translation Services _____

Appendix X
Professional Medical Organizations

- American Association of Medical Assistants (AAMA)
- American Association for Medical Transcription (AAMT)
- American College of Physicians (ACP)
- American Hospital Association (AHA)
- American Medical Association (AMA)
- American Medical Technologists (AMT)
- American Pharmaceutical Association (APhA)
- American Society of Clinical Pathologists (ASCP)
- American Society of Phlebotomy Technicians (ASPT)

Appendix XI
Medical Resources on the Internet

- American Medical Association—http://www.ama-assn.org
- Centers for Disease Control and Prevention—http://www.cdc.gov/
- E Medicine Consumer Health—http://www.emedicinehealth.com/script/main/hp.asp
- Medline Plus—http://medlineplus.gov/
- National Institutes of Health—http://www.nih.gov/
- National Library of Medicine—http://www.nlm.nih.gov/
- New England Journal of Medicine—http://content.nejm.org/
- Virtual Hospital—http://lib.cpums.edu.cn/jiepou/tupu/atlas/www.vh.org/
- WebMD—http://www.webmd.com/

Index